MW00817827

ANTICHRIST
BEFORE THE DAY OF THE LORD

ALAN KURSCHNER

ANTICHRIST
BEFORE THE DAY OF THE LORD

WHAT EVERY CHRISTIAN NEEDS TO KNOW
ABOUT THE RETURN OF CHRIST

ESCHATOS
PUBLISHING

Copyright © 2013 by Alan Kurschner

All rights reserved. No part of this publication may be reproduced, stored in a retrieval system, or transmitted in any form or by any means—for example, electronic, photocopy, recording—without the prior written permission of the publisher. The only exception is brief quotations in printed reviews.

Eschatos Publishing
P.O. Box 107
Pompton Lakes, NJ 07442

Printed in the United States of America

Publisher's Cataloging-in-Publication

    Kurschner, Alan.
       Antichrist before the day of the Lord : what every
    Christian needs to know about the return of Christ / by
    Alan Kurschner.
      pages cm
      Includes bibliographical references and index.
      LCCN 2013951163
      ISBN 978-0-9853633-0-7 (cloth)
      ISBN 978-0-9853633-1-4 (pbk.)

      1. Antichrist. 2. Rapture (Christian eschatology)
    3. End of the world.   I. Title.

    BT985.K87 2013   236
                 QBI13-600167

Unless otherwise noted, all Scripture is from the New English Translation (NET) of the Bible, copyright 1996–2013. Unless otherwise noted, all Greek definitions are from *A Greek-English Lexicon of the New Testament and Other Early Christian Literature*, rev. and ed. Fredrick W. Danker, 3rd ed. (Chicago: University of Chicago Press, 2000).

To my loving parents

Contents

Illustrations

Figures

Tables

Photographs

Acknowledgments

I want to thank Heidi Walker, my editor; Linda M. Au for interior; and Michael Coldagelli, Tom Klein, and Charles Cooper for their time in recent years giving me feedback on various issues discussed in the book. I want to thank my wife Donna for her sacrifice, who began to wonder if this book would be finished before the day of the Lord! I also want to thank the many who supported me through their prayers and financial support, for this book would not have seen the light of day without all of you.

Introduction

This book is what every Christian needs to know about the return of Christ. It is part of the larger Christian teaching called "eschatology," which comes from the Greek word *eschatos* ("last") and means "the study of last things." My goal is to focus on what the biblical writers believed were the most prominent issues related to the second coming. What are these issues and where can they be found in the Bible?

Let me take the last question first. In the Old Testament, the relevant end-time issues are found mostly in the writings of the prophets. In the New Testament, they are found in Jesus' Olivet Discourse (Matthew 24–25; Luke 21; Mark 13), Paul's teaching in the Thessalonian epistles, and, not surprisingly, the book of Revelation. Thus, these are the biblical passages I will be drawing from.

Next, what are the major issues related to the return of Christ in these passages? In this book, I will be writing from what is called the "prewrath" perspective. The prewrath position places importance on three central events related to Christ's return: (1) the Antichrist's great tribulation, which will happen just before Christ's return; (2) the rapture of God's people, which will

1

happen on the first day of Christ's return; and (3) the day of the Lord's wrath, which will begin immediately after the rapture. These three events will be treated in the three parts of this book.

Some may question why a book on Christ's return is necessary. They may take the position, "What only matters is that Jesus is returning!" This sounds pious, but it is not biblical. What it implies is that these other "side" issues regarding the great tribulation, timing of the rapture, and the day of the Lord's wrath were not concerns for the biblical writers. It may come as a surprise, however, that the biblical writers themselves did not believe that it was sufficient simply to know that Christ is returning. Indeed, Jesus *is* coming back, and there is no question that knowing this truth should propel us to holy living. But Jesus himself ominously warns us to be aware of what will happen *before* he returns: "See, I have told you beforehand" (Matt. 24:25). Jesus, Paul, and the book of Revelation consistently teach that the church will have her faith tested by the Antichrist and his persecution during the great tribulation. In the context of describing this persecution, Jesus asks, "When the Son of Man comes, will he find faith on earth?" (Luke 18:8). Paul commands, "Let no one deceive you in any way" (2 Thess. 2:3). The book of Revelation warns, "This requires the steadfast endurance of the saints—those who obey God's commandments and hold to their faith in Jesus" (Rev. 14:12). It is imperative that every believer take this seriously.

The end-time teachings of Jesus (Matthew 24–25), Paul (1, 2 Thessalonians), and the book of Revelation give prominence to the event of the Antichrist's great tribulation that will happen before Jesus returns for his church. In fact, in the Olivet Discourse, Jesus places more emphasis on how to live during the testing period before his return than on his return itself! Accordingly, we, too, must model Jesus' example by emphasizing the ramifications of the Antichrist's great tribulation upon the church. The task for the student of prophecy is to affirm not just *that* Jesus is returning but the *conditions* surrounding his return. This includes the Antichrist's persecution, the period when God will refine his bride for his Son's arrival.

This prewrath teaching may sound new—even challenging—to some. You might have grown up in a tradition that believed we will be raptured before the Antichrist's great tribulation (as I did). If this describes you, I encourage you to be a "Berean" in the faith and test everything in this book against the Word of God. "These [Bereans] were more open-minded than those in Thessalonica, for they eagerly received the message, examining the scriptures carefully every day to see if these things were so" (Acts 17:11).

Four Major Outlooks on Biblical Prophecy

Before delving into the prewrath understanding of Jesus' return, let's look at the four umbrella interpretations of the end times to provide a broader understanding of the discussion.

The first outlook, or approach, is futurism. Futurists interpret most of the events in the Olivet Discourse, 1 and 2 Thessalonians, and the book of Revelation as yet to be fulfilled. For example, futurists believe that the Antichrist and his great tribulation are still to come, an event that will occur just before Christ comes back, not an event that has already been fulfilled or that is being fulfilled at the present time. The second outlook is preterism, which believes that these events, including the Antichrist's great tribulation, have already been fulfilled. Preterism holds that these events were fulfilled in the first century in relation to the destruction of Jerusalem in A.D. 70. The third outlook is historicism, which interprets events such as the Antichrist's great tribulation as being fulfilled throughout the church age between the first and second comings of Christ (also called "inter-adventism"). The fourth outlook is idealism, which interprets these events only as symbolic or spiritual—as timeless ethical truths about the struggle between good and evil.

In this book, my approach is futurist, so I will be writing from this point of view and primarily for those who share this outlook. This is not to say that preterists, historicists, and idealists cannot benefit from this book, because some of their concerns will overlap at points with futurism.

Four Major Futurist Positions

Within the umbrella of futurism, there are four primary futurist positions—pretribulationism, midtribulationism, posttribulationism, and prewrath. One characteristic that makes these positions futurist is they affirm that there will be a future seven-year period during which the three major end-time events unfold. I will say more on this seven-year period in Part 1. All these positions also affirm that believers are promised exemption from the day of the Lord's wrath. "For God did not destine us for wrath but for gaining salvation through our Lord Jesus Christ" (1 Thess. 5:9). Accordingly, an important question for all of these positions is when the day of the Lord's wrath begins in relation to the seven-year period. The answer will inform us of where each view places the rapture in relation to the seven-year period. I will briefly outline the main tenets of each of the futurist positions.

Pretribulationism teaches that the seven-year period, which pretribulationists refer to as "the tribulation," is entirely the day of the Lord's wrath. Thus, they see the rapture as occurring just before the seven-year period begins. According to pretribulationism, the church will not face the Antichrist's great tribulation since the rapture will happen first. Pretribulationism does not make a distinction between the Antichrist's great tribulation and the day of the Lord's wrath.

Pretribulational Model

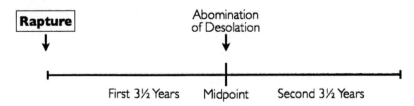

First 3½ Years   Midpoint   Second 3½ Years

(The Day of the Lord covers the entire seven years
i.e. the "Tribulation Period")

Midtribulationism has variants to its position, but at its core, it teaches that the rapture will happen at the midpoint of the seven-year period before the Antichrist's great tribulation. This position shares affinity with pretribulationism in that it sees the rapture as happening before the Antichrist's great tribulation. In recent decades, the midtribulational position has become practically defunct. I am mentioning it here for completeness' sake.

Midtribulational Model

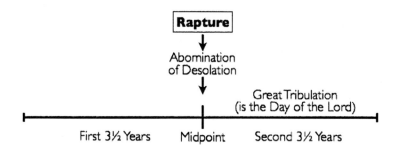

Posttribulationism teaches that the rapture will happen at the completion of the seven-year period. Some posttribulationists deny a future seven-year period, yet they still affirm that the major prophetic events will happen in the future. Unlike pretribulationism and midtribulationism, this view believes that the church will face the Antichrist's great tribulation. It holds that the day of the Lord's wrath occurs within a single twenty-four hour day at the very end of the seven-year period. (Some posttribulationists have the day of the Lord's wrath unfolding during the second three-and-one-half years as God physically protects the church on *earth* while he pours out his wrath upon the ungodly.)

Posttribulational Model

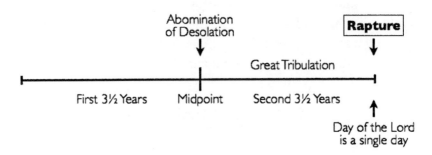

Prewrath teaches that the rapture will occur sometime during the second half of the seven-year period. We do not know the exact day or hour (Matt. 24:36). Prewrath makes an important biblical distinction between the events of the Antichrist's great tribulation and the day of the Lord's wrath. The Antichrist's great tribulation will be directed against the church, and at some unknown time, those days will be cut short with the coming of Jesus to resurrect and rapture God's people. Then God will immediately begin to pour out his day-of-the-Lord wrath against the ungodly.

Prewrath Model

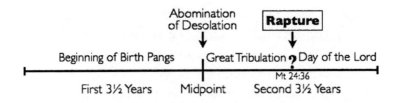

? = The question mark means that Christ's return to resurrect and rapture God's people will happen at an unknown day and hour (Matt 24:36). But it will occur sometime during the second half of the seven-year period. When the rapture occurs on that unknown day, it will cut short the Antichrist's great tribulation against believers followed by the day of the Lord's wrath against unbelievers.

Many of us were taught that the church will be "raptured out of here" *before* the Antichrist's persecution. However, as I will show in this book, the Bible consistently instructs us that the church will experience the Antichrist's great tribulation before Christ returns to rapture his people and execute his wrath upon his enemies—hence "prewrath."

PART 1.
The Antichrist's Great Tribulation

PART 1.

The Antichrist's Great Tribulation

I entitled Part 1 "The Antichrist's Great Tribulation" to high-light that this period is characterized by the Antichrist's per-secution against God's people. It is not the period of God's wrath. The Antichrist's fury will be against the church, as well as a remnant of Jews who will not capitulate to him. We will learn that the Bible makes an important distinction between the pe-riod of the Antichrist's great tribulation and the day of the Lord's wrath. The great tribulation will happen first, and it will be fol-lowed by God's judgment.

In Part 1, I will first consider some preliminaries. For exam-ple, the future Antichrist will be a literal figure, not a symbolic one. I will also show that the book of Daniel informs us of a fu-ture seven-year period (commonly called "the seventieth week of Daniel") during which key eschatological events will take place. Then I will explain the "beginning of birth pangs" that will hap-pen just before the great tribulation. Second, my focus in Part 1 will be to describe the nature and purpose of the Antichrist's great tribulation, drawing from Jesus' Olivet Discourse, Paul's Thessalonian epistles, and concluding with the book of Revela-tion.

A Literal Antichrist

There is a broad and narrow sense of the term "antichrist." The broad theological sense is defined by the apostle John, who writes, "Who is the liar but the person who denies that Jesus is the Christ? This one is the antichrist: the person who denies the Father and the Son" (1 John 2:22). A few verses earlier John prophesied of a narrow sense of an eschatological Antichrist: "Children, it is the last hour, and just as you heard that *the* antichrist is coming, so now many antichrists have appeared. We know from this that it is the last hour" (1 John 2:18, emphasis mine). So John recognizes an already-not-yet sense of antichrist ("the antichrist is coming [not yet], so now many antichrists have appeared [already]").

Two chapters later he restates this already-not-yet sense: "but every spirit that does not confess Jesus is not from God, and this is the spirit of the antichrist, which you have heard is coming, and now is already in the world" (1 John 4:3). Thus for John there is now (at the present time) the *spirit* of antichrist, and in the future an *embodiment* in a literal figure, not merely a symbolic one.

There is more evidence for a literal, personal Antichrist figure. In Matthew 24:15, Jesus personifies the "abomination of desolation" that will be "standing" [*histēmi*] in the holy place: "So when you see the abomination of desolation—spoken about by Daniel the prophet—standing in the holy place . . ." (Matt. 24:15). In Mark 13:14, the writer uses the masculine participle *hestēkota* ("standing"), which indicates that a person is in view. The apostle Paul also explicitly describes this figure as a person.

> Let no one deceive you in any way. For that day will not come, unless the rebellion comes first, and *the man* of lawlessness is revealed, *the son* of destruction, *who* opposes and exalts *himself* against every so-called god or object of worship, so that *he* takes *his* seat in the temple of God, proclaiming *himself* to be God. (2 Thess. 2:3–4 ESV, emphasis mine)

The early church believed that the Antichrist would be a literal person, as well. This is demostrated by the earliest Christian document outside the New Testament, called the Didache, "The Teaching" (pronounced DID-ah-kay). In chapter 16:4, it reads,

> For as lawlessness increases, they will hate and persecute and betray one another. And then *the deceiver of the world* will appear as *a son* of God and will perform signs and wonders, and the earth will be delivered into *his* hands, and *he* will commit abominations the likes of which have never happened before. (emphasis mine)[1]

Both Scripture and the early church show clear evidence that the Antichrist will be a real person.

Seven-Year Time Frame

The Bible teaches that a future seven-year period represents the final seven years of this age. Pretribulational teachers mistakenly equate this period with what they have coined "the tribulation period." This expression is misleading because it is vague and, as we will learn, neglects the biblical distinction between the great tribulation and the day of the Lord. Therefore, I will refer to this period using the neutral term "the seven-year period."

Why did God ordain this time frame? In Daniel 9, the prophet Daniel anguished over the sins of rebellious Israel and prayed to God, confessing on behalf of his nation and asking for mercy, forgiveness, and repentance. While Daniel was praying, God sent a prophetic word through the angel Gabriel. Daniel was told that God would take a block of 490 years out from history: "Seventy weeks [i.e. 490 years] have been determined concerning your people and your holy city to put an end to rebellion, to bring sin to completion, to atone for iniquity, to bring in perpetual righteousness, to seal up the prophetic vision, and to anoint a most holy place" (Dan. 9:24). In the generations subsequent to Daniel, the first 483 years of the 490 were fulfilled by the time of the first century; however, the last seven years remain to be fulfilled. At the conclusion of this period, the prophecy of Israel's salvation will be accomplished.

Since I am assuming a futurist approach in this book, I will not take the time here to argue for the futurity of the seven-year period.[2] However, I want to make several comments on this temporal framework. A very important verse is Daniel 9:27:

> He [the Antichrist] will confirm a covenant with many [Israel] for one week [i.e. seven years]. But in the middle of that week he will bring sacrifices and offerings to a halt. On the wing of abominations will come one who destroys, until the decreed end is poured out on the one who destroys. (cf. Dan. 12:11)

This verse states "he" will confirm a covenant with many for "one week" (*šābûa*), which in this Hebrew context denotes seven years. The New English Translation rendering "confirm" may not capture the force of the underlying Hebrew verb *gābar*. The English Standard Version renders it "make a strong covenant," which better captures the sense (cf. Ps. 12:4); but the sense behind the Hebrew may better indicate oppressing, imposing, or coercing, suggesting that the other party to the covenant may not have much say in the matter.[3] The "he" is an antichrist figure. The covenant may be for protection or permission to reinstitute the sacrificial system in return for some other service or action. It is implied that the Antichrist will break the covenant by stopping the sacrifices and offerings, causing abominations. This will occur in the middle of that week (i.e. the midpoint of the seven-year period). Accordingly, the "many" refers to Israel since the covenant relates to the stopping of the sacrifices and offerings associated with the Jewish temple. However, the "many" could also suggest that most of Israel will support the covenant, but a remnant will dissent.

A question remains: Will we recognize the signing of the covenant when it happens and thereby know that we have entered the seven-year period? I do not think we can be certain that we will. What will be unmistakable, however, is the midpoint event—the revelation of the Antichrist and his abomination of desolation. We will see that Jesus, Paul, and the book of Revelation never focus on the beginning of the seven-year period, let alone mention the signing of a covenant. The absence of these events in key New Testament passages suggests that the writers did not consider them important enough to need to focus our attention on them. Instead, all three New Testament sources stress that it is at the midpoint at which there is a discernible event by which believers will know for certain that they have entered the season of the great tribulation.

Antichrist's Seven-Year Covenant

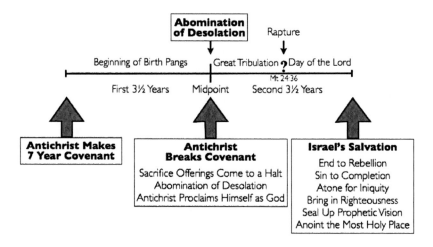

Having established a seven-year timeline, we can situate key prophetic events, including when the Antichrist will commit abominations and stop sacrifices and offerings, at the midpoint of that timeline. I will consider the nature and purpose of the Antichrist's persecution program called the great tribulation. First I will address Jesus' Olivet Discourse, followed by Paul's teaching, and conclude with the book of Revelation.

Situating Jesus' Olivet Discourse

The Olivet Discourse given on the Mount of Olives was one of Jesus' last instructions to his disciples before he was crucified.[4] The Olivet Discourse is recorded in the three synoptic gospels (Matthew 24–25, Mark 13, Luke 21). I have chosen Matthew's account since it is the fullest of all three, and I will draw from Luke's and Mark's accounts when helpful. There are seven sections to Matthew's account. In Part 1, I will cover through the great tribulation up to verse 28.

Outline of Matthew 24–25	
24:1–3	Prediction of the Temple
24:4–8	The Beginning of Birth Pangs
24:9–14	The Great Tribulation
24:15–28	The Great Tribulation Developed
24:29–31	The Day of the Lord Begins
24:32–25:30	Similes and Parables for Watchfulness
25:31–46	Sheep and Goats Judgment

In Matthew 21, there is the so-called "triumphal entry," which eventually ends in conflict between Jesus and the Scribes and Pharisees, who repeatedly challenged his authority. This culminates in Jesus pronouncing seven woes against these hypocrites, followed by his lament of the obstinate and unrepentant hearts of the Jewish leadership. Matthew 24 begins with Jesus walking away from the temple after this confrontation with the Jewish leaders, causing his disciples confusion and distress. Attempting to salvage something from the conflict, the disciples draw Jesus' attention to the splendid temple structures as if to reconcile him back to the laurels of Israel's religious achievements. But Jesus would not be taken in by such externalities. Matthew records,

Now as Jesus was going out of the temple courts and walking away, his disciples came to show him the temple buildings. And he said to them, "Do you see all these things? I tell you the truth, not one stone will be left on another. All will be torn down!" (Matt. 24:1–2)

Jesus had previously prophesied the destruction of Jerusalem (Luke 19:41–44). But now he completes this prediction by focusing on the epicenter of life in the city, the temple. The fulfillment of these two prophecies occurred a few decades later in A.D. 70 when the Romans razed Jerusalem and the temple was destroyed.

In Matthew 23:39, Jesus told the Jewish leaders he was leaving them. "For I tell you, you will not see me from now until you say, 'Blessed is the one who comes in the name of the Lord!'" This announcement and Jesus' prediction of the temple's destruction prompted the disciples to ask two questions: "Tell us, when will these things happen?" and "What will be the sign of your coming [*parousia*] and of the end of the age?" (Matt. 24:3). The Greek noun for "coming" is *parousia*, which means "an arrival and a continuing presence."[5] It is the term behind the expression "second coming" or "second advent." The Lord's second coming (*parousia*) will be a comprehensive-complex whole. In other words, it will not be a simple, instantaneous event as the rapture will be. Instead it will span various events that will fulfill divine purposes.

We can illustrate this by looking at Jesus' first coming. When we think of this event, we do not think exclusively of his birth. His birth was his arrival, but his subsequent presence included his upbringing, teaching ministry, miracles, discipling, death, burial, and resurrection. It was a complex whole that God used to fulfill his purposes. Similarly, the second coming will begin with Jesus' arrival in the clouds to resurrect the dead and rapture them along with believers who are alive at that time (1 Thess. 4:13–18). The biblical writers often emphasized the arrival aspect of the parousia because they wanted to induce godly living in their listeners. But it would be a mistake to think they viewed it as limited only to Jesus' glorious appearing in the sky to resurrect the dead and rapture all believers. This is because his subsequent presence will encompass major events such as the day of the Lord's wrath, bringing the remnant of Israel to salvation, and reclaiming his earthly regal-rule, which will extend into the millennium. In short, Christ is coming back as deliverer, judge, and king. (For more on the parousia and related terms, see the appendix "Key Terms Related to the Return of Christ.")

The Beginning of Birth Pangs

The disciples' questions imply that they assumed that the destruction of the temple buildings and the consummation of the age would be a two-fold event with both events happening about the same time. However, Jesus will challenge this preconceived notion as well as other kingdom categories. During Jesus' ministry, whenever he was asked a direct question it was common for him to ignore the question, reply with a question, or give an unexpected answer to the question that challenged the questioner's preconceived beliefs. In this case, he chooses the latter, taking the opportunity to challenge the disciples' preconceived eschatological categories, especially the kingdom of God. Jesus will teach them that deceptive temptation and great suffering must come first for those who desire to be in his kingdom at the consummation. The disciples' question elicits from Jesus one of his longest recorded teachings in the gospels, the Olivet Discourse. He opens:

> "Watch out that no one misleads you. For many will come in my name, saying, 'I am the Christ,' and they will mislead many. You will hear of wars and rumors of wars. Make sure that you are not alarmed, for this must happen, but the end is still to come. For nation will rise up in arms against nation, and kingdom against kingdom. And there will be famines and earthquakes in various places. All these things are the beginning of birth pains." (Matt. 24:4–8)

Before Jesus reveals the sign of his return (vv. 27, 30), he describes a cluster of conditions that must happen first. He cautions the disciples not to be alarmed when these things happen, thinking wrongly that the end of the age is imminent because it will be a time of tumult in the world (politically and naturally), as well as for the church (false messiahs and teachings). To describe this period, Jesus uses the metaphor "beginning of birth pangs." This period will be characterized by hardship; otherwise, his warning not to be misled or alarmed would not be meaningful. The period will not be as intense as the labor pains during the great tribulation, which Jesus says will be an unprecedented time for God's people. Nevertheless, the beginning of birth pangs will be an intensely challenging time for the church, both physically and spiritually.

When will the beginning of birth pangs take place? Preterism holds that they have already been fulfilled. In the preterist view, these events took place in the years leading up to A.D. 70. Historicism holds that these events are in the process of *being* fulfilled over time, gradually unfolding over the span of the church age. These two conclusions are unlikely because there are reasons to believe this cluster of events will occur in the future in proximity to our Lord's coming. First, the topic of the coming and the end of the age situates these events in a consummation context. Second, the text suggests that these events will occur in conjunction with each other, not piecemeal. The thrust of Jesus' words conveys an intensity of earthquakes, wars, famine, and false messiahs that comports better with the last generation of the church, not the entire church age. Occasional bouts over the span of church history would not compel Jesus to warn, "Make sure you are not alarmed, for this must happen, but the end is still to come." Third, Jesus' use of the birthing metaphor is more intelligible when a single generation is in view. The birthing process starts (beginning of birth pangs), followed by labor pains (the great tribulation), and climaxes in delivery (the return of Christ). Thus, the import of the birthing metaphor is devoid of meaning if the beginning of birth pangs is interpreted as reaching back to the first century and covering scores of generations. Finally, verse 9 reads, "*Then* they will hand you over to be persecuted and will kill you. You will be hated by all the nations because of my name." The Greek word for "then" is *tote*, which suggests that a single generation of believers will experience both the beginning of birth pangs and the persecution, making it unlikely that the beginning of birth pangs spans the church age.

The Beginning of Birth Pangs

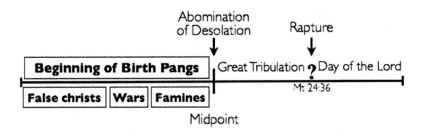

I want to make a qualification about the spectrum of interpretive certainty. On one side of the spectrum, there are those events about which we can be certain. On the other side, there are those about which we can be much less certain. Then there are points in between. I am not interested in trying to give every prophetic event the same weight of significance or certainty. The inspired biblical writers emphasized what they deemed to be important when they gave more expositional space to those matters. This is the case with the teachings of Jesus, Paul, and the book of Revelation. They consistently highlight the Antichrist's desolation of the temple and subsequent persecution of God's people during the great tribulation. At the same time, they provide minimal attention to the events preceding the great tribulation, such as—in this case—the beginning of birth pangs. Accordingly, from the prewrath perspective, we want to practice interpretative latitude upon the nature and timing of the beginning of birth pangs but give much more importance and certainty to our conclusions about the Antichrist's great tribulation, the rapture event, and the day of the Lord's wrath. To be sure, I do not think that just because some aspect is less clear or significant we should ignore it altogether. Instead, we should strive for the most likely interpretation without trying to say more than Scripture will allow us to say.

The Great Tribulation

We have seen that Jesus taught that the beginning of birth pangs is preliminary to his return, but he warned that the events that comprise it should not be mistaken to signal the arrival of the end. Now his teaching shifts to the heightened persecution of believers, the period we know as the great tribulation.

> "Then they will hand you over to be persecuted [*thlipsis*] and will kill you. You will be hated by all the nations because of my name. Then many will be led into sin, and they will betray one another and hate one another. And many false prophets will appear and deceive many, and because lawlessness will increase so much, the love of many will grow cold. But the person who endures to the end will be saved. And this gospel of the kingdom will be preached throughout the whole inhabited earth as a testimony to all the nations, and then the end will come." (Matt. 24:9–14)

This section takes the birthing imagery to its next stage, the great tribulation. Believers will face a cluster of trials and temptations that Jesus summarizes as martyrdom, hatred, apostasy, betrayal, deception, and lawlessness. In the next passage, starting at verse 15, we will see that Jesus relates back to verses 9–14, developing the great tribulation by describing how and when martyrdom will be brought about. But at this point (vv. 9–14), Jesus warns of the future onset of persecution and martyrdom. This warning

extends to the church at large since the disciples are representative of the church: "You will be hated by all the nations because
of my name." Believers are persecuted and put to death because
of Jesus' name, for his name represents the gospel, a gospel the
world hates. Even today, the mere mention of the name "Jesus"
is met with animosity in public discourse. This will reach a cre-
scendo just before Christ returns, expressed through universal
persecution and martyrdom.

Next, we are told "many will be led into sin, and they will
betray one another and hate one another." These three acts will
likely be committed by the same persons. The expression "led
into sin" refers to apostasy (cf. Mark 4:17; 14:27, 29). The pressure of persecution will be too much for them, showing them
to be only professors of the faith, not true believers. To avoid
persecution, many rationalizations and creative pretexts will be
made. Yet they will not be content with their apostasy for they
will betray and hate one another (cf. Mark 13:12). During this
time, Jesus will not suspend his command,

> "If anyone wants to become my follower, he must deny him-
> self, take up his cross, and follow me. For whoever wants to
> save his life will lose it, but whoever loses his life for my sake
> and for the gospel will save it." (Mark 8:34–35)

Jesus also prophesies that many false prophets will appear
and deceive many (cf. vv. 4–5). It is likely that those who
apostatize will fall prey to these false prophets. In addition,
Jesus says the love of many will grow cold because of a surge
in lawlessness. This "many" in verse 12 may be referring to the
"many" in verse 11 who will be led into sin or apostasy. Verse 12
also states, "lawlessness will increase so much." Literally, it can
read, "lawlessness being made complete," which implies a climax
of lawlessness. In the parable of the wheat and weeds, Jesus
says those who commit lawlessness at the end of the age will
be destroyed. "So just as the tares are gathered up and burned
with fire, so shall it be at the end of the age. The Son of Man will

send forth His angels, and they will gather out of His kingdom all stumbling blocks, and those who commit lawlessness" (Matt. 13:40–41 NASB).

Paul uses the same term for "lawlessness" (*anomia*) to refer to the climax or completion of lawlessness embodied in the Antichrist. "Let no one deceive you in any way. For that day will not come, unless the rebellion comes first, and the man of lawlessness is revealed, the son of destruction" (2 Thess. 2:3 ESV). Paul connects the man of lawlessness with the rebellion. Some translations render "rebellion" as "apostasy," since the Greek term behind it is *apostasia*. Later, we will have more to say on Paul's teaching on this point. In short, Jesus and Paul are indicating that the cause of the eschatological apostasy is related to the fulfillment of lawlessness.

In verse 13, Jesus promises, "But the person who endures to the end will be saved." In this context, he is not speaking of spiritual salvation but physical deliverance. Those who survive to the end will be delivered, as we will learn, through the rapture (Matt. 24:31; cf. 1 Thess. 4:17).

The Great Tribulation Developed

"So when you see the abomination of desolation—spoken about by Daniel the prophet—standing in the holy place (let the reader understand), then those in Judea must flee to the mountains. The one on the roof must not come down to take anything out of his house, and the one in the field must not turn back to get his cloak. Woe to those who are pregnant and to those who are nursing their babies in those days! Pray that your flight may not be in winter or on a Sabbath. For then there will be great suffering unlike anything that has happened from the beginning of the world until now, or ever will happen. And if those days had not been cut short, no one would be saved. But for the sake of the elect those days will be cut short. Then if anyone says to you, 'Look, here is the Christ!' or 'There he is!' do not believe him. For false messiahs and false prophets will appear and perform great signs and wonders to deceive, if possible, even the elect. Remember, I have told you ahead of time. So then, if someone says to you, 'Look, he is in the wilderness,' do not go out, or 'Look, he is in the inner rooms,' do not believe him. For just like the lightning comes from the east and flashes to the west, so the coming of the Son of Man will be. Wherever the corpse is, there the vultures will gather." (Matt. 24:15–28)

Verse 15 is one of the most important structural verses in the Olivet Discourse. It introduces a parenthetical section clarifying and unpacking the previous passage: "So when you see the abomination of desolation—spoken about by Daniel the prophet—standing in the holy place." In other words, verses 15–28 do not sequentially follow verses 9–14; instead, they thematically *develop* verses 9–14 on the tribulation, persecution, and spiritual action the believer is to take. We know this to be the case for a couple of reasons. Most importantly, verse 15 begins with the conjunction "so" (*oun*), which some Bible versions render "therefore." This conjunction functions inferentially as a "deduction, conclusion, or summary to the preceding discussion."[6] A second reason for the parenthetical nature is that the audience in verses 15–28 is the same as the audience before verse 15. Jesus uses the second person "you" consistently without any hint that he has two different groups of believers in view. The same "you" in verse 9 is the same "you" in verse 15 (see also vv. 20–26). There is a final reason for the parenthetical nature in verses 15–28. While verses 9–14 give a general or "shotgun" description of events that will precede the end of the age, verses 15–28 draw attention to the spiritual response of the believer who will experience the events.

The Great Tribulation

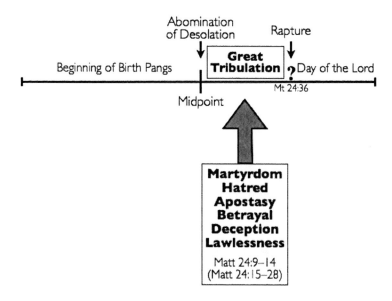

Jesus uses the expression "the abomination of desolation" to portray a personification of the Antichrist: "So when you see the abomination of desolation—spoken about by Daniel the prophet—standing in the holy place" (Matt. 24:15). Drawing from the prophet Daniel, Jesus uses this expression to personify the Antichrist as a detestable idol that causes sacrilege (Dan. 9:27, 12:11). We should recall that with Jesus referring to this verse, he is establishing a point of reference at the midpoint of the seven-year period (cf. Dan 9:27).

As noted earlier, the apostle Paul gives this desolating Antichrist figure the epithet "man of lawlessness" (2 Thess. 2:3–4; see also Dan. 7:25; 11:36). The book of Revelation uses the imagery "beast," developing more on his desolating actions.

> One of the beast's heads appeared to have been killed, but the lethal wound had been healed. And the whole world followed the beast in amazement; they worshiped the dragon because he had given ruling authority to the beast, and they worshiped

the beast too, saying: "Who is like the beast?" and "Who is able to make war against him?" The beast was given a mouth speaking proud words and blasphemies, and he was permitted to exercise ruling authority for forty-two months. So the beast opened his mouth to blaspheme against God—to blaspheme both his name and his dwelling place, that is, those who dwell in heaven. (Rev. 13:3–6)

In light of these desolating actions, we understand why Jesus says this will initiate an unequaled time of persecution. "For then there will be great tribulation, such as has not been from the beginning of the world until now, no, and never will be" (Matt. 24:21 ESV). The Greek word for "tribulation" is *thlipsis,* which denotes one or more of the following experiences: tribulation, pressure, affliction, trouble, suffering, and persecution.[7] It should be noted that this term was used as well to describe a woman's birth pangs. Previously, Jesus spoke of the "beginning birth pangs" (v. 8), but now the birthing stage is intensified to "great [*megas*] tribulation." In general, the godly and ungodly can experience *thlipsis,* but for different reasons. Jesus says the nature of being a follower of Christ will require this experience. "I have said these things to you, that in me you may have peace. In the world you will have tribulation [*thlipsis*]. But take heart; I have overcome the world" (John 16:33). By contrast, the apostle Paul warns that the ungodly will experience *thlipsis* as a result of God's wrath. "[B]ut wrath and anger to those who live in selfish ambition and do not obey the truth but follow unrighteousness. There will be affliction [*thlipsis*] and distress on everyone who does evil, on the Jew first and also the Greek" (Rom. 2:8–9).

In our eschatological context in Matthew 24, the Antichrist's great tribulation will be directed against—not the ungodly—but believers (v. 22). Revelation consistently echoes Jesus' teaching concerning this brutal period.

The beast was permitted to go to war against the saints and conquer them. He was given ruling authority over every tribe,

people, language, and nation, and all those who live on the
earth will worship the beast, everyone whose name has not
been written since the foundation of the world in the book of
life belonging to the Lamb who was killed. If anyone has an
ear, he had better listen! If anyone is meant for captivity, into
captivity he will go. If anyone is to be killed by the sword, then
by the sword he must be killed. This requires steadfast endurance and faith from the saints. (Rev. 13:7–10)

So great will this martyrdom be that Jesus says, "If those days
had not been cut short, no one would be saved. But for the sake
of the elect those days will be cut short" (Matt. 24:22; cf. 2 Thess.
1:7). In the same vein, Paul says God's people in the midst of
eschatological persecution will be given "rest" when the Lord returns. "[A]nd to you who are being afflicted to give rest together
with us when the Lord Jesus is revealed from heaven with his
mighty angels" (2 Thess. 1:7). It is no wonder that the fifth seal
martyrs cry out to God, "How long, Sovereign Master, holy and
true, before you judge those who live on the earth and avenge
our blood?" (Rev. 6:10).

Persecution, however, will not be the only adversity for God's
people during the great tribulation. It will be compounded by
deceptive temptation to capitulate to false teachings.

Deception during the Great Tribulation

False messiahs and prophets will use deceptive signs and wonders to try to convince people to follow them. But Jesus exhorts,

"Then if anyone says to you, 'Look, here is the Christ!' or
'There he is!' do not believe him. For false messiahs and false
prophets will appear and perform great signs and wonders to
deceive, if possible, even the elect. Remember, I have told you
ahead of time. So then, if someone says to you, 'Look, he is
in the wilderness,' do not go out, or 'Look, he is in the inner
rooms,' do not believe him." (Matt. 24:23–26)

The rise of these false christs and false prophets will not be a phenomenon to take lightly. Jesus prophesies that they will use persuasion (but "do not believe him") and deceit ("I have told you ahead of time"). This will be so great a temptation that, according to Jesus, if it were possible to deceive even the elect, it would happen. The temptation against God's people will be real and strong. The fact they are believers (the elect) does not excuse them from their human responsibility to resist and stay faithful. Through these warnings, God will work his persevering grace to protect them from apostasy (cf. Phil. 1:6; 1 Thess. 5:23–24; 1 Cor. 10:13; John 6:39; John 10:28–29; 1 Pet. 1:5–6).[8]

Paul on the Apostasy and Revelation of the Antichrist

In his second epistle to the Thessalonians, the apostle Paul links false teaching and apostasy to the revelation of the Antichrist. Since Paul's instruction on this subject is one of the most important in the Bible, we will devote adequate space to it.

> Now regarding the arrival of our Lord Jesus Christ and our being gathered to be with him, we ask you, brothers and sisters, not to be easily shaken from your composure or disturbed by any kind of spirit or message or letter allegedly from us, to the effect that the day of the Lord is already here. Let no one deceive you in any way. For that day will not arrive until the rebellion comes and the man of lawlessness is revealed, the son of destruction. He opposes and exalts himself above every so-called god or object of worship, and as a result he takes his seat in God's temple, displaying himself as God. Surely you recall that I used to tell you these things while I was still with you. And so you know what holds him back, so that he will be revealed in his own time. For the hidden power of lawlessness is already at work. However, the one who holds him back will do so until he is taken out of the way, and then the lawless one will be revealed, whom the Lord will destroy by the breath of his mouth and wipe out by the manifestation of his arrival.

The arrival of the lawless one will be by Satan's working with all kinds of miracles and signs and false wonders, and with every kind of evil deception directed against those who are perishing, because they found no place in their hearts for the truth so as to be saved. (2 Thess. 2:1–10)

Back in 2 Thessalonians 1, Paul encouraged the Thessalonian believers to persevere in adversity, reassuring them that these tribulations are not the eschatological day of the Lord's judgment and that God will deliver his people unto rest and glorification at Christ's revelation. Continuing this topic of the day of the Lord into 2 Thessalonians 2, Paul gives additional reassurance to the Thessalonians that they are not experiencing the day of the Lord's wrath. He will do this by describing two prophesied events that must happen before the day of the Lord. In chapter 1, Paul stresses that the day of the Lord *will come*; in chapter 2, he stresses that the day of the Lord *has not come*.

Beginning in verse 1, Paul writes,

Now regarding the arrival of our Lord Jesus Christ and our being gathered to be with him. (2 Thess. 2:1)

He links two events with each other: "the arrival of our Lord Jesus Christ" and "our being gathered." The term for "arrival" is *parousia*. Some other translations render this as "coming," but the rendering "arrival" emphasizes the starting point for the parousia, and by extension, it carries the notion of an ongoing presence. The expression "our being gathered" (*episynagōgē*) recalls Paul's previous teaching on the rapture (1 Thess. 4:15–18; cf. 2 Thess. 1:7). More on this latter point in Part 2.

The Parousia and the Gathering

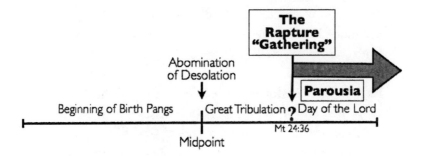

Next, Paul exhorts,

> [We ask you, brothers and sisters,] not to be easily shaken from your composure or disturbed by any kind of spirit or message or letter allegedly from us, to the effect that the day of the Lord is already here. (2 Thess. 2:2)

In this verse, Paul describes the aforementioned gathering and parousia as "the day of the Lord." It was brought to Paul's attention that the Thessalonians had come to erroneously believe that the day of the Lord had already commenced. This jolts Paul into pleading with them not to be "easily shaken from your composure or disturbed." This expression covers the intellectual and emotional aspects of a person. The only other time in the New Testament that the verb "disturbed" (*throeō*) occurs is in a strikingly similar context in the Olivet Discourse:

> "For many will come in my name, saying, 'I am the Christ,' and they will mislead many. You will hear of wars and rumors of wars. Make sure that you are not alarmed [*throeō*], for this must happen, but the end is still to come." (Matt. 24:5–6; cf. Mark 13:7)

The parallel between Jesus and Paul is interesting because both warn their listeners not to be deceived when certain events happen lest they think the Lord had already come. The false teachers in Thessalonica did not deny a day of the Lord—they affirmed it. Their error was teaching that it was happening already. In these parallel passages, we see both Jesus and Paul referencing false christ(s) who will claim authority. Since Paul had previously taught that the Thessalonians would be delivered from the Lord's wrath (1 Thess. 5:9), we can imagine their frightened state of mind thinking they had been left for judgment. Paul must combat this false teaching immediately.

The mistaken eschatology by the Thessalonian believers in 2 Thessalonians 2:2 was anticipated by Paul in 2 Thessalonians 1:5–10, where he laid a foundation of hope, teaching that they would be delivered at the revelation of Christ before the day of the Lord's judgment. In short, since the revelation of Christ had not occurred, the Thessalonians can be certain that the day of the Lord's wrath had not arrived either. Paul then provides additional certitude of this truth by explaining that two events must happen first.

> Let no one deceive you in any way. For that day will not come, unless the rebellion comes first, and the man of lawlessness is revealed, the son of destruction, who opposes and exalts himself against every so-called god or object of worship, so that he takes his seat in the temple of God, proclaiming himself to be God. (2 Thess. 2:3–4 ESV)

Paul begins by using strong language, warning the Thessalonians not to be deceived or misled through any manner. The reason why they—and by extension all Christians—should not be deceived is because the day of the Lord will not happen until two events happen first: (1) the rebellion comes, and (2) the man of lawlessness is revealed. Some have misunderstood this to mean that the rebellion will be the first event and the revelation of the man of lawlessness will be the second. But Paul does not make this sequential argument. He lumps these two related events together, instructing that both must occur before the day of the

Lord. The context will give us clues to the relationship between the rebellion and the revelation of the Antichrist.

Without elaborating on its precise nature, Paul simply states that "the rebellion" (*ho apostasia*) must come. Other translations, which I prefer, render it as "the apostasy," a term better capturing the nuance. The Greek term means a "defiance of established system or authority, rebellion, abandonment, breach of faith." This can be abandonment of either political or religious convictions. In our context, it indicates the latter, religious apostasy. But what sort of religious apostasy does Paul have in mind? This has led to various proposals.

1. *The apostasy is a conspicuous increase in ungodliness (or rebellion) within the world at large.* It is true that there will be an increase of ungodliness in the world before Christ's return (2 Tim. 3:1–9), but I think the particular apostasy Paul mentions will be narrower in scope. In the Greek, it is significant that there is an article before "apostasy" because it points to a more discernible event rather than a general apostasy.[9] Moreover, since the term for "apostasy" (*apostasia*) indicates a previously affirmed allegiance (in our context, to God), this would not describe the ungodly world at large.

2. *The apostasy will be true believers losing their salvation.* This view is inconsistent with the statement Paul makes a little later on: "But we ought to thank God always for you, brothers and sisters loved by the Lord, because God chose you from the beginning for salvation through sanctification by the Spirit and faith in the truth" (2 Thess. 2:13). For Paul, the chosen of God will be brought "for salvation." This is why Paul can thank God, because God's elect will persevere. Claiming to be a Christian does not make one a Christian. Those who claim to be Christians and later reject the faith are by definition apostate and thereby shown to be false professors of the faith.

3. *The apostasy will be Jewish in scope.* One could make a case that Jews will apostatize when they make a covenant with the Antichrist or worship the Antichrist at his revelation at the midpoint, much as they apostatized at the imposition of Antiochus IV (cf. 1 Macc. 2:15). But I do not believe it is probable that this is what this passage is referring to because it does not limit the apostasy to the Jews. Neither will it be entirely Gentile in scope. It is unlikely that the apostasy will be exclusive to a particular ethnicity.

4. *The apostasy will be the eschatological professing church.* I think this view (which sees a significant apostasy happening within the professing church at the Antichrist's coming) is the most plausible. There will be a separating out of unbelievers from believers in the church. There are two reasons I believe this to be the right interpretation. First, in our context *apostasia* is associated with an eschatological, Satan-inspired rejection of the truth, especially seen in verses 9–12 (cf. 1 Tim. 4:1; Matt. 24:9–13, 23–26). In the immediate context, we find a cluster of expressions of the Christian faith and truth from which Paul exhorts the Thessalonians not to depart:

   - "not to be easily shaken from your composure or disturbed" (v. 2)
   - "Let no one deceive you in any way" (v. 3)
   - "they found no place in their hearts for the truth" (v. 10)
   - "Consequently God sends on them a deluding influence" (v. 11)
   - "through sanctification by the Spirit and faith in the truth" (v. 13)
   - "stand firm and hold on to the traditions that we taught you" (v. 15)

The second reason relates to the prophesied event that must occur before the day of the Lord, the Antichrist's revelation (*apokalyptō*, which means "to cause something to be fully known, reveal, disclose, bring to light, make fully known"). Paul associates the Satan-inspired apostasy with the revelation of the Antichrist. In turn, he associates the Antichrist's revelation with the time he "opposes and exalts himself above every so-called god or object of worship, and as a result he takes his seat in God's temple, *displaying himself as God*" (2 Thess. 2:4, emphasis mine). Since the Antichrist will demand that the world worship him, his demand establishes an unambiguous test for those who claim to be Christians: the choice to apostatize or stay faithful. The Antichrist will become the "object of worship," with false-professing Christians apostatizing their empty faith. In short, the apostasy will be devilish, discernible, deceptive, and damning.

Next, why does Paul use the epithet "the man of lawlessness [*anomia*]" for the Antichrist? Because the Antichrist will oppose God's law. So much so, he "opposes and exalts himself above every so-called god or object of worship." The Antichrist will not just be *a* man of lawlessness but *the* man of lawlessness, making him the ultimate embodiment of lawlessness in human history. Paul then piles on another epithet for the Antichrist: "the son of destruction," which means he is destined for destruction (cf. v. 8; Rev. 17:8, 11). To be sure, there is a "hidden power" of lawlessness already at work at this time (2 Thess. 2:7), but it will one day manifest into a physical, literal individual.

The Midpoint Events of the Seven-Year Period

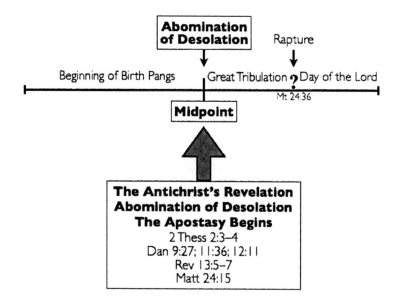

A Rebuilt Temple

Paul associates the Antichrist's revelation with him taking "his seat in God's temple, displaying himself as God." Thus, a temple will have to be rebuilt if he is to take his seat there. To be sure, the temple that will be rebuilt before the midpoint of the seven-year period will not be divinely sanctioned, for it will be part of an attempt to reinstate the old Mosaic system. Presumably, the rebuilding will be spearheaded by Orthodox Jews seeking to reestablish a holy place for Levitical sacrifices and other temple rituals prescribed in the Torah.

It is often assumed by some interpreters that, in order to fulfill this prophecy, a colossal Solomonic-like temple complex must be rebuilt. This is not the case. The term for "temple" in verse 4 is *naos*, which does not require a large temple-complex. It can refer to something much simpler, such as a tent-like structure or the inner sanctuary. Such a structure could be erected in a matter of weeks, or less. Just over one hundred years ago, it would have been difficult to fathom a reconstituted state of Israel back in their land. Nevertheless, as part of God's providential purposes, it did happen in 1948. This event should inspire confidence that, sometime in the future, a Jewish temple will be rebuilt, as well. Currently, Islam's Dome of the Rock is located on the Temple Mount, making fulfillment of this prophecy very difficult to imagine. However, with God all things are possible. Perhaps a peace accord between Israel and Muslims will permit Orthodox Jews to build a sanctuary beside (or even upon) the Temple Mount. However it will materialize, I accept the plain reading of Scripture that there will one day be a literal temple structure, and when the Antichrist is revealed, he will appropriate the temple for his own blasphemous glory.[10]

Michael, the Restrainer

> And so you know what holds him back, so that he will be revealed in his own time. For the hidden power of lawlessness is already at work. However, the one who holds him back will do so until he is taken out of the way. (2 Thess. 2:6–7)

Paul reminds the Thessalonians that they know about the restraining ministry against the Antichrist's revelation: "And so you know what holds him back." I will outline the direction of Paul's argument on this topic.

The Thessalonians were under the false impression that the day of the Lord was occurring at the time of Paul's writing. To correct their error, Paul instructs that, before the Lord's revelation happens, the Antichrist's revelation will occur first. But Paul explains that, even before the Antichrist's revelation, the individual who restrains this revelation must be first taken away. Paul describes the Antichrist's revelation as being restrained at this time, implying that God's sovereign purpose will unfold at the appointed time: "so that [the Antichrist] will be revealed in his own time." Then Paul explains that the principle of the hidden power of lawlessness is already in the world even though the man of lawlessness has not been revealed. "For the hidden power of lawlessness is already at work." Some translations render "hidden power" as "mystery." This hidden power of lawlessness will one day go unhindered. "[T]he one who holds him back will do so until he is taken out of the way." This tells us there is a figure who is restraining the embodiment of lawlessness, but in due time his restraining ministry will cease. The concealed power of lawlessness will then become the disclosed power of lawlessness embodied in the man of lawlessness, the Antichrist. Traditionally, the enigmatic figure who restrains has been properly designated "the restrainer." Once the restrainer is removed, this causes the Antichrist to be revealed, eventuating in the Antichrist taking his seat in the temple and proclaiming himself as God (2 Thess. 2:4). When this happens at the midpoint, the unabated great tribulation will commence. The book of Revelation records:

> But woe to the earth and the sea because the devil has come down to you! He is filled with terrible anger, for he knows that he only has a little time! [the great tribulation]. . . . So the dragon became enraged at the woman [the Jewish remnant] and went away to make war on the rest of her children, those who keep God's commandments and hold to the testimony about Jesus [the church]. (Rev. 12:12, 17)

Sequence of Key Events

Over the centuries, various theories have been propounded attempting to identify the restrainer. To name a few: the Holy Spirit, God the Father, the universal church, government, the Roman Empire, and the preaching of the gospel. And there are interpreters who have thrown up their hands and claimed an impasse to the restrainer quest. Recently, however, there has been ground-breaking research on this topic by Thessalonian scholar Colin R. Nicholl. He contends that the "restrainer" Paul is referring to is Michael the Archangel. Here is an outline of his arguments.[11]

1. In contemporary Jewish literature, the characteristics used to describe Michael establish him as having eschatological preeminence as the chief opponent of Satan and restrainer of God's people.

2. Michael is viewed as a celestial restrainer of God's people in Daniel 10–12, the larger passage that serves as the source for Paul's exposition in 2 Thessalonians 2:3–8.

3. Daniel's use of the Hebrew verb ʿmḏ in Daniel 12:1 comports with the ceasing activity of the restrainer in 2 Thessalonians 2:6–7.

4. The Greek term *parerchomai* in Daniel 12:1 of the Septuagint (LXX) means "to pass by," which shows that ancient Jewish interpretation of this text viewed Michael ceasing his restraint at this eschatological event. Instructing on the restrainer in 2 Thessalonians 2:6–7, Paul is most likely drawing from Daniel's text.

5. Early Rabbinic interpretation of Daniel 12:1 conveyed Michael as "passing aside" or "withdrawing" in relation to the Antichrist's establishment near or at the Temple Mount (Dan. 11:45) and just before the unequaled, eschatological tribulation against God's people (Dan. 12:1).

6. Revelation 12:7–17 supports viewing Michael as the restrainer because it links Michael's heavenly war against the dragon with the eschatological persecution of God's people (cf. 2 Thess. 2:6–7; Dan. 11:45–12:1).

These reasons strongly suggest that in 2 Thessalonians 2:6–7 the apostle Paul sees Michael the Archangel as the restrainer, whose ministry ceases and causes the eschatological temple to be desolated by the Antichrist, an event that is ensued by the Antichrist's great tribulation against God's people.

The Antichrist's Ultimate Destruction

[When the restrainer is removed] then that lawless one will be revealed whom the Lord will slay with the breath of His mouth and bring to an end by the appearance of His coming. (2 Thess 2:8 NASB)

Paul only mentions the Antichrist coming to his end when the Lord returns. He does not describe the complex series of parousia judgments that debilitate the Antichrist's power and lead to his final demise; for this we have to look elsewhere. The book of Revelation, as we will later see, shows that the trumpet and bowl judgments diminish the Antichrist's power, with the battle of Armageddon bringing about his ultimate demise.

> Then I saw the beast and the kings of the earth and their armies assembled to do battle with the one who rode the horse and with his army. Now the beast was seized, and along with him the false prophet who had performed the signs on his behalf—signs by which he deceived those who had received the mark of the beast and those who worshiped his image. Both of them were thrown alive into the lake of fire burning with sulfur. (Rev. 19:19–20)

Antichrist's Phased-Out Reign

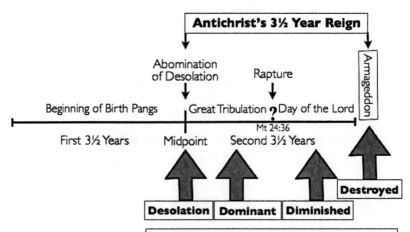

Antichrist is given authority to persecute saints for 3½ years. However, his ability to persecute is diminished during the day of the Lord's wrath. Antichrist will be finally destroyed at Armageddon by being thrown into the lake of fire.

Satanic Possession and Deceptive Miracles

I would be remiss if I gave the Antichrist too much credit for his opposition against God. The real enemy is Satan, who has been opposed to God ever since the garden of Eden. In the garden, Satan deceived our first parents, but he will deceive the entire world in his eschatological possession of the man of lawlessness.

> The arrival of the lawless one will be by Satan's working with all kinds of miracles and signs and false wonders, and with every kind of evil deception directed against those who are perishing, because they found no place in their hearts for the truth so as to be saved. (2 Thess. 2:9–10; cf. Rev. 12:12, 17)

Paul gives this parenthetical description of Satan's intentions and his means of attempting to achieve his diabolical goal. The revelation of the Antichrist will be a key event for Satan's purposes. Certainly the world is not going to worship an individual simply because he claims to be God. False believers will not apostatize without a powerful deception and real threat. There must be something that convinces the world—albeit deceptively—to give him their allegiance.

Out of the twenty-four instances of the term *parousia* in the New Testament, 2 Thessalonians 2:9 is the only one that refers to the Antichrist's parousia, rendered here as "arrival." It will not be that the Antichrist's coming is merely influenced by Satan; rather, the expression "by Satan's working [*energeia*]" conveys Satanic *possession*. Satan will use deceptive "miracles and signs and false wonders" (cf. Mark 13:22). This will help the Antichrist position himself with power and credibility when he takes his seat in the temple proclaiming himself to be God. George Eldon Ladd captures this well when he says,

> The manifestations of evil which have marked human history will at the end of the age be concentrated in one final incar-nation of evil, a "super-man," the Antichrist, who will exer-

cise a world-wide rule, deify the state and achieve a union of church and state so that men will be forced to worship him or suffer economic sanctions and death. Antichrist, energized by satanic powers, will especially direct his hostility against God and the people of God. During his ascendency, there will befall God's people the most fearful persecution history has witnessed.[12]

In conclusion, Paul has given us one of the clearest passages in all of Scripture instructing that the church will be here during the period of the Antichrist. The Thessalonians needed to be taught that the Lord's return had not yet occurred—the Antichrist and the apostasy must come first. Pretribulationism, which claims that the rapture will occur before the Antichrist, renders Paul's teaching unintelligible, making his warnings to the Thessalonians a mere academic exercise. Not to mention, if the day of the Lord starts at the beginning of the seven-year period as pretribulationists claim, then it makes no sense that Paul would give prominence to the revelation of the Antichrist that happens at the midpoint.

Paul directs his teaching to believers because the deception through the Antichrist will be experienced by the last generation of the church. If the church is to be raptured before the Antichrist, why does Paul so passionately warn believers concerning the Antichrist's deception at his revelation? He could have simply told them that the day of the Lord cannot happen until the rapture occurs first. Instead Paul instructs them that the revelation of the Antichrist and the apostasy are evidence that the day of the Lord—and by extension being "gathered" to Christ at the rapture—has not yet come because he expects the last generation of the church to see it transpire. Since we have not seen the revelation of the Antichrist and the apostasy, the Lord has not returned; therefore, there is no need to be "shaken from your composure or disturbed."

Two Related Events *Before* the Day of the Lord

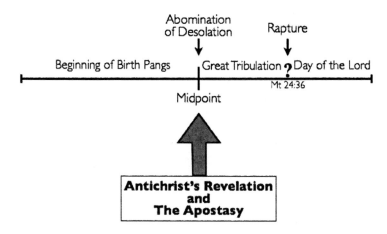

Book of Revelation on the Two Great Acts of Deception

Revelation 13 gives us a fuller composite of Satan's activity behind the great tribulation. The italicized words highlight the supernatural satanic causes.

> Then I saw a beast coming up out of the sea. It had ten horns and seven heads, and on its horns were ten diadem crowns, and on its heads a blasphemous name. Now the beast that I saw was like a leopard, but its feet were like a bear's, and its mouth was like a lion's mouth. *The dragon gave the beast his power, his throne, and great authority to rule.* One of the beast's heads appeared to have been killed, but *the lethal wound had been healed.* And *the whole world followed the beast in amazement;* they worshiped the dragon because *he had given ruling authority to the beast,* and they worshiped the beast too, saying: "Who is like the beast?" and "Who is able to make war against him?" The beast was *given a mouth speaking proud words and blasphemies,* and he was permitted to exercise ruling author-

ity for forty-two months. So the beast opened his mouth to blaspheme against God—to blaspheme both his name and his dwelling place, that is, those who dwell in heaven. The beast was permitted to go to war against the saints and conquer them. He was given ruling authority over every tribe, people, language, and nation, and all those who live on the earth will worship the beast, everyone whose name has not been written since the foundation of the world in the book of life belonging to the Lamb who was killed. If anyone has an ear, he had better listen! If anyone is meant for captivity, into captivity he will go. If anyone is to be killed by the sword, then by the sword he must be killed. This requires steadfast endurance and faith from the saints. Then I saw another beast coming up from the earth. He had two horns like a lamb, but was speaking like a dragon. He exercised all the ruling authority of the first beast on his behalf, and made the earth and those who inhabit it worship the first beast, the one whose lethal wound had been healed. *He performed momentous signs, even making fire come down from heaven in front of people and, by the signs he was permitted to perform on behalf of the beast, he deceived those who live on the earth.* He told those who live on the earth to make an image to the beast who had been wounded by the sword, but still lived. *The second beast was empowered to give life to the image of the first beast so that it could speak, and could cause all those who did not worship the image of the beast to be killed.* He also caused everyone (small and great, rich and poor, free and slave) to obtain a mark on their right hand or on their forehead. Thus no one was allowed to buy or sell things unless he bore the mark of the beast—that is, his name or his number. This calls for wisdom: Let the one who has insight calculate the beast's number, for it is man's number, and his number is 666. (Rev. 13:1–18, emphasis mine)

This passage teaches that there will be two great acts of deception for the purpose of inducing the world to worship the Antichrist.

First is the counterfeit resurrection of the Antichrist:

> One of the beast's heads appeared to have been killed, but the lethal wound had been healed. And the whole world followed the beast in amazement; they worshiped the dragon because he had given ruling authority to the beast, and they worshiped the beast too, saying: "Who is like the beast?" and "Who is able to make war against him?" (Rev. 13:3–4)

Second is the false prophet performing supernatural signs:

> He exercised all the ruling authority of the first beast on his behalf, and made the earth and those who inhabit it worship the first beast, the one whose lethal wound had been healed. He performed momentous signs, even making fire come down from heaven in front of people and, by the signs he was permitted to perform on behalf of the beast, he deceived those who live on the earth. (Rev. 13:12–14)

These two acts of deception will not be David Copperfield magic. They will be genuine Satan-inspired signs intended to deceive the world into worshiping the Antichrist and thus Satan himself. The instruments that Satan and the Antichrist will impose upon the world to guarantee worship are the twofold image and mark. The most notorious and enigmatic passage in the book of Revelation reads,

> He told those who live on the earth to make an image to the beast who had been wounded by the sword, but still lived. The second beast was empowered to give life to the image of the first beast so that it could speak, and could cause all those who did not worship the image of the beast to be killed. He also caused everyone (small and great, rich and poor, free and slave) to obtain a mark on their right hand or on their forehead. Thus no one was allowed to buy or sell things unless he bore the mark of the beast—that is, his name or his number.

This calls for wisdom: Let the one who has insight calculate the beast's number, for it is man's number, and his number is 666. (Rev. 13:14–18)

The choice is clear: Partake of the Antichrist's unholy sacrament and live under his short-lived reign or refuse his worship and be killed for Christ's name and live under Christ's reign forever. God will not accept any exceptions for those who capitulate by taking the mark. The following solemn pronouncement should put the fear of God into any Spirit-filled believer:

A third angel followed the first two, declaring in a loud voice: "If anyone worships the beast and his image, and takes the mark on his forehead or his hand, that person will also drink of the wine of God's anger that has been mixed undiluted in the cup of his wrath, and he will be tortured with fire and sulfur in front of the holy angels and in front of the Lamb. And the smoke from their torture will go up forever and ever, and those who worship the beast and his image will have no rest day or night, along with anyone who receives the mark of his name." This requires the steadfast endurance of the saints— those who obey God's commandments and hold to their faith in Jesus. (Rev. 14:9–12)

Situating the Seven Seals

In the final section of Part 1, I want to conclude by highlighting from the book of Revelation the fourth and fifth seals, which depict martyrs dying during the great tribulation. But first we will preface some comments on the first three seals. (For the structure of the book of Revelation, see the appendix "Proposed Structure to the Book of Revelation.")

The book of Revelation describes a scroll sealed with seven "seals" that are conditions required for the scroll to be opened and the contents of the day of the Lord's wrath to be executed as expressed through the trumpet and bowl judgments.[13] There is a logical progression in the seven seals. As I will argue below, the most plausible scenario is that the first three seals occur during the first half of the seven-year period *before* the great tribulation; the fourth and fifth seals occur *during* the great tribulation; the sixth seal occurs toward the *end* of the great tribulation, signaling the impending day of the Lord; and the seventh seal occurs immediately *after* the great tribulation, pronouncing the day of the Lord's wrath.

We should, however, recognize a spectrum of certainty in this progression. What do I mean by this? Concerning the first three seals, I think we are least certain as to when they will occur during (maybe even before) the seven-year period. My purpose in this section is to focus on the fourth and fifth seals, which we are more certain about, as they are happening during the great tribulation. Since the Antichrist's revelation occurs during the great tribulation, which is the focal event in this book, I will keep my comments on the first three seals to a minimum. In Parts 2 and 3, I will address the last two seals, the sixth and the seventh, about which we possess the greatest degree of certainty since they close out the great tribulation and introduce the day of the Lord's wrath, respectively.

Seven Seals Unfolding in the Seven-Year Period

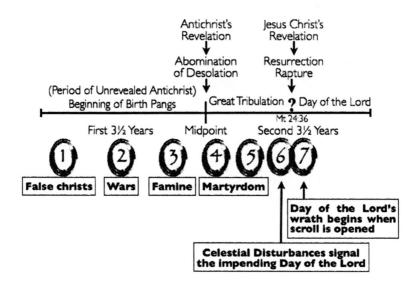

John records the portrayal of the first three seals,

> I looked on when the Lamb opened one of the seven seals, and
> I heard one of the four living creatures saying with a thunder-
> ous voice, "Come!" So I looked, and here came a white horse!
> The one who rode it had a bow, and he was given a crown,
> and as a conqueror he rode out to conquer. Then when the
> Lamb opened the second seal, I heard the second living crea-
> ture saying, "Come!" And another horse, fiery red, came out,
> and the one who rode it was granted permission to take peace
> from the earth, so that people would butcher one another, and
> he was given a huge sword. Then when the Lamb opened the
> third seal I heard the third living creature saying, "Come!" So
> I looked, and here came a black horse! The one who rode it
> had a balance scale in his hand. Then I heard something like
> a voice from among the four living creatures saying, "A quart
> of wheat will cost a day's pay and three quarts of barley will
> cost a day's pay. But do not damage the olive oil and the wine!"
> (Rev. 6:1–6)

As a preface, it should be noted that these first three seals parallel
the beginning of birth pangs in Jesus' Olivet Discourse (see Matt.
24:4–8). But the parallels will not stop there. In our study, we will
further learn that the other seals correspond to the sequence in
Jesus' teaching, as well.

The first seal is the most ambiguous of the seven. Certainly
there is an emerging conquering figure, but who is he? Various
proposals have been offered, the two most common candidates
being Christ and the Antichrist. I think there are good reasons
to see the first seal as representing the Antichrist, not Christ.[14]
If it does represent the Antichrist, it would not represent him
at the time of his revelation at the midpoint but most likely as
he comes on the political scene at the beginning of the seven-
year period when he is still unrevealed to the world. If this is
correct, then it adds support to the view that the second, third,
and fourth seals are phases of the Antichrist's campaign, with

the fourth seal representing his persecution program during the great tribulation.

The second seal (wars and rumors of wars) may symbolize a military phase in the Antichrist's campaign, reflecting the time when he establishes himself as a military world leader, consolidating his power base. The fiery red color of the horse likely represents bloodshed since the second seal indicates international wars (he will "take peace from the earth"). Throughout history, there have always been wars here and there, including world wars, but the language associated with the second seal conveys an intensification of war, perhaps a world war on an unprecedented scale.

The third seal results in famine and scarcity, which may be the consequence of battle in the war-torn areas the Antichrist conquers. The black horse of this seal symbolizes famine. The imagery of a balance scale symbolizes high prices and rationing of food due to scarcity (cf. Ezek. 4:16; Lev. 36:26). Another indication of famine is that the writer of Revelation describes the value of the wheat and barley as eight to sixteen times the average prices in the Roman Empire at the time. In an eschatological context, this will be inflation to an acute degree.[15] This food crisis may allow the Antichrist to assert his control over food prices and related commodities. How would he eventually do this? Presumably, the crisis would carry over into the second half of the seven-year period, and when the Antichrist institutes his mark-of-the-beast scheme, he will use it to assume absolute control of who can buy and sell.

The Fourth Seal—Means of Killing

Then when the Lamb opened the fourth seal I heard the voice of the fourth living creature saying, "Come!" So I looked and here came a pale green horse! The name of the one who rode it was Death, and Hades followed right behind. They were given authority over a fourth of the earth, to kill its population with the sword, famine, and disease, and by the wild animals of the earth. (Rev. 6:7–8)

The fourth and most certainly the fifth seal represent martyrdom during the great tribulation. It is my contention that the fourth seal reflects the consequences of refusing to take the Antichrist's mark. This will be a dark time for believers. They will need to trust God completely for physical and spiritual sustenance (Matt. 6:25–34). The fourth seal shifts perspective from the world at large to a more limited scope. This final horse is pale green, symbolizing death, personified by the final rider with Hades following him. Authority was given to these two personified, malevolent forces by God's permission to kill by various means—sword, famine, pestilence, and wild beasts of the earth.[16] This authority is limited to "over a fourth of the earth." To be sure, the expression "to kill" suggests intention. It doesn't mean that this intention is accomplished. In contrast, the book of Revelation will actually state when such a massive number of people are killed; for example, "A third of humanity was killed by these three plagues, that is, by the fire, the smoke, and the sulfur that came out of their mouths" (Rev. 9:18; cf. 11:13). The question is whether one-fourth of the earth is geographic or demographic. The fourth seal is not clear on this point. However, the fifth seal is likely a result of the fourth seal; but we should not assume that one-fourth of the earth are martyrs. It may refer just to Christendom in general. Nevertheless, the Antichrist will likely control the entire globe politically and religiously (Rev. 13:3, 7–8; Dan. 7:23); but in God's sovereignty, his intent to kill may be restricted. In this context, the fourth seal would be the means of killing (*apokteinō*) and the fifth seal would be the result (*apokteinō*).

Next, the passage says that Death and Hades will use "wild beasts of the earth" to kill. It is significant that the term for "beasts" (*thērion*) is used thirty-nine times in the book of Revelation. In every instance, it refers to the Antichrist or his associations (his image, system, or religious accomplice). This is the first time the term is used. Since it refers to the Antichrist and his associations in the remaining thirty-eight instances, it would be very unusual, though not impossible, for it not to refer to the Antichrist and his religious associations here, as well. In addition, there is a definite article "the" (*ho*) that precedes "beasts," which makes the beasts *definite*. In other words, it is not referring to beasts as a general class; instead, the presence of the article indicates particularity.[17] Later we learn that the book of Revelation explicitly states that the beast is, in fact, responsible for putting believers to death. "If anyone is meant for captivity, into captivity he will go. If anyone is to be killed by the sword, then by the sword he must be killed. This requires steadfast endurance and faith from the saints" (Rev. 13:10; cf. Rev. 20:4).

It is not surprising that "Hades" is said to follow close behind "Death." A combination of Old Testament usage of these terms reveals that they are basically synonymous (e.g. Psalm 6:5; 49:14; 116:3; Prov. 2:18; 5:5; 7:27; Job 33:22; 38:17). Another connection between the paired Antichrist and false prophet with Death and Hades is that both pairs are thrown into the lake of fire (Rev. 19:20; 20:10, 14).

In light of these observations, I suggest that the fourth seal represents a choice people must make. In the book of Revelation, the overarching choice for everyone on earth is to follow the Antichrist or Jesus Christ (cf. Revelation 13; 14:9–13). Those who follow Christ risk death by "sword, famine-pestilence, and by wild beasts," the consequences for not following the Antichrist.

The Fifth Seal—Result of Killing and the Promise of God's Wrath

> Now when the Lamb opened the fifth seal, I saw under the altar the souls of those who had been violently killed because of the word of God and because of the testimony they had given. They cried out with a loud voice, "How long, Sovereign Master, holy and true, before you judge those who live on the earth and avenge our blood?" Each of them was given a long white robe and they were told to rest for a little longer, until the full number was reached of both their fellow servants and their brothers who were going to be killed just as they had been. (Rev. 6:9–11)

The fifth seal depicts the result *and* the ongoing killings of the Antichrist. The martyrs are portrayed as crying out for justice concerning their wrongful deaths, asking their sovereign God when his wrath will be poured out to vindicate them. John sees "under the altar the souls of those who had been violently killed because of the word of God and because of the testimony they had given" (Rev. 6:9).

The fifth seal is problematic for the pretribulational interpretation, which sees all the seals as expressions of the day of the Lord's wrath. However, the fifth seal explicitly applies to believers, not unbelievers. To be more specific, it applies to *martyred* believers! The pretribulational interpretation by necessity has believers suffering the wrath of God. This contradicts the biblical promise that believers will not experience God's wrath. "For God did not destine us for wrath but for gaining salvation through our Lord Jesus Christ" (1 Thess. 5:9).

In addition, the fifth seal clearly states that, even at the time of their martyrdom, the wrath of God is yet future.

> They cried out with a loud voice, "How long, Sovereign Master, holy and true, *before you judge* those who live on the earth and avenge our blood?" Each of them was given a long white robe and they were told to *rest for a little longer, until* the full number was reached of both their fellow servants and their brothers who were going to be killed just as they had been. (Rev. 6:10–11, emphasis mine)

The fifth seal martyrs recognize that they did not die as a result of God's wrath; instead they are crying out to God asking when he will avenge their blood. This is confirmed with a heavenly promise that God's wrath will occur very soon; but before this onset, the providential fulfillment of martyrdom must be reached. In the meantime, martyred souls are given long white robes and told "to rest for a little longer." Long white robes are a guarantee of the resurrection hope soon to take place. In Part 2, we will see that, after the sixth seal is opened, this resurrection promise is fulfilled: "an enormous crowd that no one could count, made up of persons from every nation, tribe, people, and language, standing before the throne and before the Lamb dressed in long white robes" (Rev. 7:9, cf. vv. 13–14).

The fifth seal is pivotal because, while it is the goal of the Antichrist to kill Christians, the giving of white robes points to God's impending vindication. Thus we need to recall the Lord's command: "Do not avenge yourselves, dear friends, but give place to God's wrath, for it is written, 'Vengeance is mine, I will repay,' says the Lord" (Rom. 12:19; cf. Luke 18:7–8).

The Antichrist's Woes, then God's Wrath	
Seals 1–4	The Woes: False Christs, War, Famine, Martyrdom
Seal 5	Effect of the Woes: Result of Martyrdom
Seal 6	Signaling God's Wrath: Celestial Disturbances
Seal 7	God's Expressed Wrath: Trumpets and Bowls

God's Good Purposes in Suffering

In light of all this discussion about God's people being killed for their faith, inevitably the question arises: What good purposes does God have in this dreadful event? Why would God have his beloved people face the Antichrist? It is an honest question.

God in his wisdom has ordained the last generation of the church to experience an unprecedented global persecution, and it could be our generation. His purpose is to purify his church, for he is coming back for a blameless bride who will have "steadfast endurance" in faith even through terrible suffering. It is difficult sometimes for believers to understand God's righteousness and love in light of his authorization of malevolent horsemen to inflict suffering upon his own people. Yet his love and righteousness are maintained if we understand that he has an ultimately good purpose behind it. Certainly, ordaining his people to suffer will not be anything new during the great tribulation. Joseph experienced unspeakable injustice, yet he recognized that God ordained it for an all-wise and good purpose: "As for you, you meant to harm me, *but God intended it for a good purpose*, so he could preserve the lives of many people, as you can see this day" (Gen. 50:20, emphasis mine). Another example is God's redemption of his people through the most intense and unjust suffering anyone could ever experience: the crucifixion of his Son, Jesus. We are taught explicitly this was ordained by the will of God (Acts 2:23; 4:27–28). We may not know at the time why God brings suffering and trials into our lives. But during them, we are called to trust his all-wise, all-good, and all-loving purposes. Job humbly recognized God's sovereign purposes as he suffered, saying, "Indeed, I am completely unworthy—how could I reply to you? I put my hand over my mouth to silence myself" (Job 40:4).

The first four seals—especially the fourth—will purify the remnant's faith. Blessings of freedom and comfort can easily breed complacency and external religiosity, of which Israel frequently testified in the Old Testament. Consequently, God brought comparable judgments upon Jerusalem. "For this is what the sovereign Lord says: How much worse will it be when I send my four terrible judgments—sword, famine, wild animals, and plague—to Jerusalem to kill both people and animals!" (Ezek. 14:21; cf. Lev. 26:18–29, Deut. 32:23–27). These judgments had an aim to purify his people from their rebellious condition and bring them to repentance (cf. Ezek. 14:22–23).

To be sure, Christians are under no condemnation from God since they are forgiven and justified. This does not mean, however, that God will not test and refine the church with suffering, as he has done in the past. It is God's prerogative—and loving purpose—to purify his people before his return (1 Thess. 3:13; 5:23; 1 Cor. 1:8; Phil. 1:10; Eph. 5:27). This will not be a time to fear but to faithfully stand firm for the occasion to bring glory to God in suffering and overcoming, no matter the cost (1 Pet. 4:12–19).[18]

Conclusion

In Part 1, I started by explaining some preliminaries about the Antichrist and situating his actions in a seven-year period. The Antichrist's revelation will occur at the midpoint, followed by his great tribulation against the church. The warning to the church is not to apostatize; instead we are called to persevere in faith during the unequaled persecution and acute deception. After I expounded on Jesus' and Paul's instructions on the great tribulation, I concluded with an explanation of the first five seals in the book of Revelation, focusing on the fourth and the fifth seals. In Part 2, "The Rapture of God's People," I will show that a unique cluster of celestial events will signal to the world God's impending wrath, as well as signal to the church her impending deliverance. During this celestial upheaval and blackout, the great tribulation will be cut short with the Lord's brilliant return in the clouds to resurrect his people and deliver those who have remained alive up to his return, rapturing both groups to meet him in the air.

Part 2.
The Rapture of God's People

Part 2.
The Rapture of God's People

At some point toward the end of the great tribulation a cluster of unique celestial disturbances will cause an upheaval and global blackout. Then the Lord will radiantly return in the clouds to resurrect his people and deliver believers who remain alive, rapturing both groups to meet him in the air. In Part 2, I will first consider this unique cluster of celestial disturbances that will signal to the church her impending deliverance from the great tribulation and signal to the world God's impending wrath. Then I will focus on the rapture event in passages from Jesus, Paul, and the book of Revelation. Each contributes an important element to the larger picture of God's eschatological deliverance.

The Great Tribulation 'Cut Short'

In God's providential timing, he will "cut short" the great tribulation for the sake of the elect. This cutting short, we will see, is by means of the rapture. Jesus prophesies,

> "For then there will be great suffering unlike anything that has happened from the beginning of the world until now, or ever

> will happen. And if those days had not been cut short, no one would be saved [i.e. delivered]. But for the sake of the elect those days will be cut short." (Matt. 24:21–22)

The expression "those days" is not denoting literal days, as if each twenty-four-hour day is itself shortened, for example, to a twenty-hour day. Nor does it mean that the seven-year period is shortened. Rather, the phrase "those days" refers to the time of persecution. The great tribulation against believers will be cut short, otherwise "no one would be saved." This cutting short is by means of physical deliverance, not spiritual salvation. The New American Standard Bible has a better rendering: "no life would have been saved." If the persecution were allowed to reach the Antichrist's intended goal, every believer would be exterminated. Jesus reveals the purpose for the shortening: "for the sake of the elect" (cf. v. 31). The Greek term for "cut short" is *koloboō,* which means "to reduce the duration of something, shorten," and can generally connote amputating or preventing something from reaching its full-intended length. When the Antichrist's great tribulation is cut short, it will allow sufficient time for God to unleash his day-of-the-Lord wrath throughout the remainder of the seven-year period, which includes, for example, the fifth trumpet judgment that lasts five months (Rev. 9:5).

In relation to the second half of the seven-year period, exactly when will this cutting short (resulting from the coming of Christ) occur? We cannot know because Jesus says, "But as for that day and hour no one knows it—not even the angels in heaven—except the Father alone" (Matt. 24:36). What we can know, however, is that the great tribulation begins at the midpoint of the seven years when the Antichrist causes an abomination of desolation, setting himself up in a temple-like structure and commanding the world to worship him (cf. Dan. 9:27; 2 Thess. 2:3–4). Accordingly, the most we can know is that the cutting short will happen *sometime during the second half of the seven-year period* because the second coming will commence sometime during that time. But we will not know the day nor the hour.[19]

The Great Tribulation 'Cut Short'

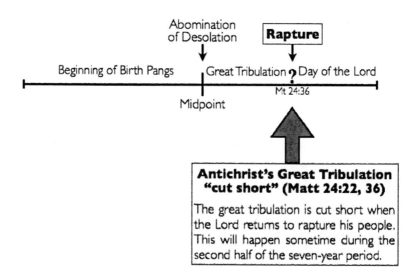

The Celestial Disturbance Event

The celestial disturbance is a frequent theme in the Bible, so it is incumbent upon us to pay attention to what it is trying to tell us. Christ is not just going to arrive on the clouds without any warning to the world. He will use a harbinger to announce his impending judgment and deliverance. This celestial event will be anything but inconspicuous, for the Lord will use the heavenly bodies to cause a celestial salvo.

> "Immediately after the suffering of those days, the sun will be darkened, and the moon will not give its light; the stars will fall from heaven, and the powers of heaven will be shaken." (Matt. 24:29)

Most certainly Jesus has in mind Joel's prophecy of an explicit sign to the eschatological day of the Lord.

I will produce portents both in the sky and on the earth—
blood, fire, and columns of smoke. The sunlight will be turned
to darkness and the moon to the color of blood, before the day
of the Lord comes—that great and terrible day! (Joel 2:30–31;
cf. Isa. 13:9–10)

Joel provides us with what is called the *terminus a quo*, which
means the earliest possible starting point for something. In our
case, Joel reveals that the day of the Lord cannot begin until
these celestial disturbances happen first—*before* the day of the
Lord. In the past, God used celestial signs to mark out seasons
and other events, including a celestial sign to the first coming of
Christ (Matt. 2:2). Joel does not intend this celestial event to be
confused with an ordinary, isolated occurrence such as a solar or
lunar eclipse. This will be a *cluster* of disturbed celestial bodies
portending the impending wrath of God. It will be unprecedented so the world will not mistake it.

Celestial Sign Announces the Day of the Lord

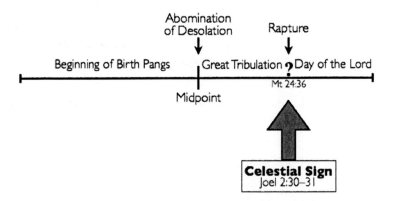

While Joel explicitly specifies that this celestial disturbance
will signal the day of the Lord, Jesus adds another piece of information. Matthew 24:29 begins with "*immediately after* the suf-

fering of those days." What days? The days of great tribulation (v. 21). When God cuts short the days of great tribulation (v. 22), the celestial disturbances will begin immediately.

A question remains as to the nature of these celestial disturbances. There have been various speculations, from a literalistic extreme saying the moon will actually turn to blood and the sun will literally burn out to the opposite extreme claiming that the language is only figurative, symbolizing God's power. Both of these views possess imbalance. The literalistic interpretation is flawed because Joel does not say that the moon will actually turn into blood. It says the moon will turn to the "*color* of blood." Likewise, Jesus does not state that the moon will disappear. He states that the "moon will not give its *light.*" Further, if the sun burns out, humanity would perish immediately. The same goes for stars falling from the sky, which would consume the earth in their path. This celestial imagery is not intended for an extreme literal interpretation. It is phenomenological language—that is, from our human perspective. So, what will be the exact nature of these celestial events? It is likely that the falling stars refer to meteors and the moon turning blood red and the sun darkening will be caused by an earthly cataclysmic disaster, possibly volcanoes (or worse, a singular super volcano). In any case, it will not be a single celestial event. It will be multiple events functioning together as a salvo of havoc, signaling the day of the Lord as unmistakable.

The other interpretive extreme, spiritualization, is not tenable either because it denies the material realization of these events, symbolizing them only as a "concept" of God's power. Certainly the celestial disturbances convey God's power, but it will be power materialized in a real, historical event. This is evident in Luke's account.

> "And there will be signs in the sun and moon and stars, and on the earth nations will be in distress, anxious over the roaring of the sea and the surging waves. People will be fainting from fear and from the expectation of what is coming on the world,

for the powers of the heavens will be shaken. Then they will see the Son of Man arriving in a cloud with power and great glory. But when these things begin to happen, stand up and raise your heads, because your redemption is drawing near." (Luke 21:25–28)

Luke highlights that there will be polar responses to the celestial disturbance event from two types of people. The ungodly will be in "distress, anxious . . . fainting from fear and from the expectation of what is coming on the world." The godly, however, are exhorted to "stand up and raise your heads, because your redemption is drawing near." The spiritualizing of the celestial phenomenon does not work because these two groups are responding to *real events*, not merely to a concept.

Luke also develops the celestial composite picture by adding an earthly element. He records Jesus as saying, "and on the earth nations will be in distress, anxious over the roaring of the sea and the surging waves." Nations do not distress over mere ten-foot waves, so this suggests a global impact. Waves of terrifying size may be caused by meteors crashing into the seas, or this may be tsunami language. Interestingly, the Greek term for "surging waves" (*salos*) can mean "earthquake." For a tsunami to cause distress on a global scale, it would have to be caused by a gigantic earthquake or a cluster of regional earthquakes. So, more descriptively, we could call the sign to the day of the Lord's wrath the "earthly-celestial" disturbances.

The Sixth Seal Signals Impending Wrath

This leads us to our final (and most descriptive) celestial passage of the sixth seal found in the book of Revelation.

Then I looked when the Lamb opened the sixth seal, and a huge earthquake took place; the sun became as black as sackcloth made of hair, and the full moon became blood red; and the stars in the sky fell to the earth like a fig tree dropping its unripe figs when shaken by a fierce wind. The sky was split apart like a scroll being rolled up, and every mountain and island was moved from its place. Then the kings of the earth, the very important people, the generals, the rich, the powerful, and everyone, slave and free, hid themselves in the caves and among the rocks of the mountains. They said to the mountains and to the rocks, "Fall on us and hide us from the face of the one who is seated on the throne and from the wrath of the Lamb, because the great day of their wrath has come, and who is able to withstand it?" (Rev. 6:12–17)

When the sixth seal is opened, an immense earthquake will take place, adding an earthly element to these unmistakable and global visible signs. This earthquake will likely be universally felt, portending Yahweh's coming to judge the earth. Perhaps it is the cause of what appear to be global tsunamis in Luke's account (Luke 21:25–27). This same earthquake may also be alluded to by the prophet Isaiah.

The one who runs away from the sound of the terror will fall into the pit; the one who climbs out of the pit, will be trapped by the snare. For the floodgates of the heavens are opened up and the foundations of the earth shake. The earth is broken in pieces, the earth is ripped to shreds, the earth shakes violently. The earth will stagger around like a drunk; it will sway back and forth like a hut in a windstorm. Its sin will weigh it down, and it will fall and never get up again. (Isa. 24:18–20; cf. vv. 21–23)

John uses ominous imagery to describe the sixth seal. "The sun became as black as sackcloth made of hair, and the full moon became blood red." Sackcloth was a coarse material made of black goat's hair, symbolizing soberness and mourning. What will the ungodly be mourning for? Their very lives! The moon will turn an ominously blood-red color. Most likely, the same event causing the sun to darken will also cause the darkening of the moon. The celestial lights will go dark, preparing for the luminous divine-glory to radiate the globe.

Another heavenly element that our Revelation passage portends is the falling of celestial bodies. "The stars in the sky fell to the earth like a fig tree dropping its unripe figs when shaken by a fierce wind." This language may indicate an unprecedented meteor shower. It will be accompanied by the sky being "split apart like a scroll being rolled up, and every mountain and island was moved from its place." This language can also describe the sky that "could no longer be seen [*apochōrizō*]."[20] This exceptional imagery of the sky splitting apart or disappearing probably serves the purpose of disclosing to the ungodly the presence of God in heaven, for in the very next sentence the ungodly cry, "Hide us from the face of the one who is seated on the throne and from the wrath of the Lamb." The term for "face" is *prosōpon*, which can mean a literal face or someone's personal presence. This "presence," combined with the upheaval all around them, will cause them to try to flee from God. So, during the sixth seal, God will split the sky to disclose his presence from heaven to be seen by the ungodly. This event is classically apocalyptic. The sky splitting apart, certainly, would be one of the most jaw-dropping elements in this celestial overture. This will pave the way for Jesus' descent from heaven to gather his people to himself (Matt. 24:30; cf. 1 Thess. 4:16–17; Acts 1:11; Rev. 1:7).

In the last event, "every mountain and island was moved from its place." If meteors hit the earth, it is not surprising that the impact—compounded by a great earthquake—will affect land masses such as mountains and islands. The question is whether the mountains and islands will be moved or actually *removed* from their places. The term for "moved" is *kineō*, which contains a range of nuances. I am more inclined to interpret this as devastating the islands and mountains, but not to the degree of annihilation. It is only at the climactic seventh bowl judgment that we find a more intense earthquake described (cf. Rev. 16:18–20). In response to the sixth-seal upheaval, John narrates the reaction of the ungodly:

Then the kings of the earth, the very important people, the generals, the rich, the powerful, and everyone, slave and free, hid themselves in the caves and among the rocks of the mountains. They said to the mountains and to the rocks, "Fall on us and hide us from the face of the one who is seated on the throne and from the wrath of the Lamb, because the great day of their wrath has come, and who is able to withstand it?" (Rev. 6:15–17)

This reaction recalls Luke's account of how they will respond: "fainting from fear and from the expectation of what is coming on the world, for the powers of the heavens will be shaken" (Luke 21:26). The sixth seal also alludes to Isaiah:

Go up into the rocky cliffs, hide in the ground. Get away from the dreadful judgment of the Lord, from his royal splendor! Proud men will be brought low, arrogant men will be humiliated; the Lord alone will be exalted in that day. (Isa. 2:10–11; cf. vv. 19–21)

This upheaval will affect the gamut of social classes, showing no preferential treatment for anyone. Social status will not save anyone from God's wrath at the end of their lives. The ungodly will not interpret the sixth seal as naturally freakish. They will see it as portending *divine retribution*. In verses 15–17, the ungodly try to hide—even asking to be killed—so as to escape the impending wrath (*orgē*) of God. The human response to this eschatological theophany finds a parallel in our first parents during the primal day-of-the-Lord theophany: "and they hid from the Lord God among the trees of the orchard" (Gen. 3:8). The response from the ungodly to the sound of the coming of Yahweh has always been to run and hide from his righteous face. It happened in the garden, and it will again, globally.

If God calls you to live in the last generation of the church to encounter the Antichrist's great tribulation, what will your reaction be to this cataclysmic celestial disturbance that shakes the heavens? Will you "faint from terror, apprehensive of what is coming on the world"? Or, as I hope, will you be faithful and confident to "stand up and lift up your heads, because your redemption is drawing near"?

By comparing Scripture with Scripture, we have been able to establish a composite picture of this celestial event. The consistency among Joel, Jesus, and the book of Revelation demonstrates that this event signals the looming day of the Lord. It will engender two opposite reactions: terror for the wicked and triumph for the godly. Only when this celestial condition occurs will the rapture event actually be imminent. Not before then! The rapture of God's people is the event we will take up next.

Composite of the Celestial Disturbance Event

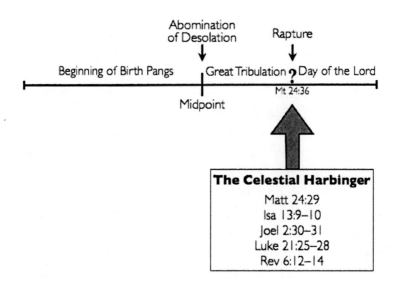

Shekinah Sign and Jesus Arriving on the Clouds

Up to Matthew 24:27, Jesus has not answered the disciples' question about the sign of his coming and the end of the age (cf. Matt.

24:3). Jesus prophesied about the preliminary birth pangs that will affect the world at large, and he warned his disciples that great suffering for God's people would precede his return. Now, in verse 27, he finally reveals the specific sign of his coming: "For just like the lightning comes from the east and flashes to the west, so the coming of the Son of Man will be." This verse begins with "for" (*gar*), which gives the reason the disciples are not to believe people when they say, "Here is the Christ!" or "There he is!" (cf. Matt. 24:23–26). The lightning imagery denotes his Shekinah glory, the radiant glory of his divine presence (cf. "His lightning bolts light up the world; the earth sees and trembles" Ps. 97:4). When it happens, there will be no need to point it out because it will be unmistakable. The directional analogy of flashing from the east to the west indicates the universal visibility of the event. The Shekinah glory will be the authenticating sign of the genuine Messiah, contrasting it with false messianic claimants.

In conjunction with Jesus explaining the sign, he ominously utters the proverb, "Wherever the corpse is, there the vultures will gather" (Matt. 24:28). This verse is related to what came before it and what comes after it. It is a pivotal structural verse in that it distinguishes two epochs of human history, conveying the principle that where moral corruption exists, divine judgment is required. When the world's depravity has reached full to the brim, God's eschatological judgment will begin. This comports with the narrative structure of Matthew 24 because everything preceding verse 28 describes moral corruption, and everything following it describes divine judgment. In short, the proverb serves as a warning that the day of the Lord's judgment will begin when Christ returns. There may be an additional point to this proverb, as well. People will no more miss the presence of the Son of Man when he returns than vultures will miss the presence of corpses. Jesus' return will be obvious.

At some point during the celestial spine-chilling darkness, global-seismic quakes, and tempestuous seas, the Lord will pierce through in all of his theophanic, Shekinah splendor.

"Then the sign of the Son of Man will appear in heaven, and all the tribes of the earth will mourn. They will see the Son of Man arriving on the clouds of heaven with power and great glory." (Matt. 24:30)

This parousia-glory authenticates Christ's presence, contrary to the false signs originating from inauthentic christs. To accentuate the brilliant sign, the Shekinah glory is revealed against the backdrop of the dark celestial disturbances. (Other related verses that mention Christ's appearance are 1 Timothy 6:14; 2 Timothy 4:8; Titus 2:13; Acts 2:20; 1 John 2:28; 1 John 3:2; Colossians 3:4; 1 Peter 5:4; and Revelation 1:7.) The Greek term for "heaven" (*ouranos*) in this context refers to the sky rather than the abode of God because it depicts Jesus' descent with clouds. That the nations ("tribes") of the earth will see him indicates that this is not a localized event but a global appearance (cf. Rev. 1:7). The nations will not repent. They will mourn, knowing that Jesus is coming as judge. The clouds are vehicles of transportation. In antiquity they were a cachet of deity—Jesus is the divine cloud-rider. His appearance at his return will be the *par excellence* of theophanies, for it will be the global and definitive revelation bringing this present age to completion. It will be the fulfillment of a promise given at his ascension.

After he had said this, while they were watching, he was lifted up and a cloud hid him from their sight. As they were still staring into the sky while he was going, suddenly two men in white clothing stood near them and said, "Men of Galilee, why do you stand here looking up into the sky? This same Jesus who has been taken up from you into heaven will come back in the same way you saw him go into heaven." (Acts 1:9–11)

Christ's return at his second coming will contrast with the events of his first coming in another way, as well:

1. In the first coming of Christ, the celestial sign announcing the coming of the Lord was *peaceful* (Matt. 2:2, 7, 9–10).

2. In the second coming of Christ, the celestial sign announcing the coming of the Lord will bring *upheaval* (Joel 2:30–31; Matt. 24:29).

Another contrast is the Shekinah sign of Christ:

1. At the first coming of Christ, Jesus' glory was *concealed* in humiliation: "This will be a sign for you: You will find a baby wrapped in strips of cloth and lying in a manger" (Luke 2:12).

2. At the second coming of Christ, Jesus' glory will be *revealed* in exaltation: "For just like the lightning comes from the east and flashes to the west, so the coming of the Son of Man will be" (Matt. 24:27; cf. 30).

The Sign to the Parousia

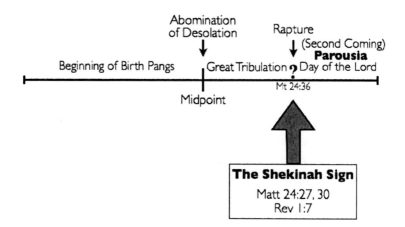

'Gather His Elect'

The celestial disturbance event will signal to the entire world the impending day of the Lord. This will be followed by the glorious-manifestation sign of Christ's coming when he descends through the sky. At this point, the great tribulation is cut short when Jesus' angels "gather his elect."

> "And he will send his angels with a loud trumpet blast, and they will gather his elect from the four winds, from one end of heaven to the other." (Matt. 24:31)

At Christ's ascension, he scattered his elect witnesses to the corners of the earth. "But you will receive power when the Holy Spirit has come upon you, and you will be my witnesses in Jerusalem, and in all Judea and Samaria, and to the farthest parts of the earth" (Acts 1:8). At his second coming, Jesus will gather the fruit of his disciples' labor, God's people, from the four winds of the heavens to his presence.

Prewrath contends that the "gather his elect" event in verse 31 is a reference to the rapture, which also includes the resurrection. Not everyone agrees, however, including pretribulational and preterist interpreters. Pretribulational theology places the rapture before the great tribulation. They interpret this gathering as the physical gathering of Jews back to the land of Israel when Jesus returns. To be sure, prewrath affirms that there will be a gathering of Jews back to the land of Israel, but it will not happen at this point. Preterist theology interprets this gathering as an event already begun or completed near the year A.D. 70. In contrast to pretribulationism and preterism, prewrath believes that the weight of evidence supports this gathering to be the rapture.

The expression "gather his elect" is an implicit expression, lacking specificity. It was not Jesus' purpose in his Olivet Discourse to expand on this event. The disciples were asking for the identification *of the sign itself*, not what would happen after the sign. I will later consider four reasons why verse 31 is a reference to the rapture. But first we need to walk through the most explicit rapture passage in the Bible given by the apostle Paul in his first epistle to the Thessalonians. This will inform our understanding of the gathering event in Matthew 24:31. This approach makes sense because Paul draws from Jesus' Olivet Discourse for his own teaching in his Thessalonian epistles (see the appendix "Parallels between Jesus and Paul").

Situating the Thessalonian Letters

> Now we do not want you to be uninformed, brothers and sisters, about those who are asleep, so that you will not grieve like the rest who have no hope. For if we believe that Jesus died and rose again, so also we believe that God will bring with him those who have fallen asleep as Christians. For we tell you this by the word of the Lord, that we who are alive, who are left until the coming of the Lord, will surely not go ahead of those who have fallen asleep. For the Lord himself will come down from heaven with a shout of command, with the voice of the archangel, and with the trumpet of God, and the dead in Christ will rise first. Then we who are alive, who are left, will be suddenly caught up together with them in the clouds to meet the Lord in the air. And so we will always be with the Lord. Therefore encourage one another with these words. (1 Thess. 4:13–18)

The apostle Paul's letters are replete with teachings on the Lord's coming. Most often they are brief passages scattered throughout his thirteen letters with an occasional larger section. Yet he wrote two letters with the exclusive purpose of answering eschatological concerns: the Thessalonian letters. Thessalonica was located in ancient Macedonia, which is present-day Thessaloniki, Greece. Paul visited this city on his second missionary journey and there planted a church that was mostly Gentile. Both of his epistles to this church may have been his first, written about A.D. 50–51. I want to consider Paul's teaching on the classic rapture passage in 1 Thessalonians 4:13–18. Even though this is a popular rapture passage, we should keep in mind the historical concern Paul is addressing: that the Thessalonians are grieving hopelessly like the pagans.

Correct Eschatology Matters

Sometime after Paul left Thessalonica, he received a report from Timothy on the situation of the church (1 Thess. 3:6). Presumably, this report contained information that some members had died, causing angst within the church about their destiny since they would not be alive at the Lord's coming. Paul writes back to reassure these new believers that they will be reunited with their deceased loved ones at the parousia. He begins his reassurance, writing,

> Now we do not want you to be uninformed, brothers and sisters, about those who are asleep, so that you will not grieve like the rest who have no hope. (1 Thess. 4:13)

This verse is the most important verse in the epistle because it informs us that Paul's purpose for writing to the grieving Thessalonians was to respond to their ignorance of the relationship between the resurrection and the parousia of Christ. If Paul can accomplish the goal of correcting this ignorance, he believes that the Thessalonians should be comforted in their distress because their manner of grieving is inconsistent with Christian hope.

The ignorance of the Thessalonians prompts Paul to stress that their deceased are not at a disadvantage. It will not only be the survivors at the coming who will be delivered, but the dead in Christ as well. Their loved ones will not only participate in the return of Christ, but they will have the privilege of coming with Christ (as disembodied souls); thereby, the dead in Christ will have the blessing of participating in God's first divine purpose at Christ's parousia, the resurrection. At that time, there will be a reunion of the dead in Christ and the alive in Christ who have survived. Therefore they need to stop grieving like their pagan neighbors who do not possess this certain hope. Paul writes,

> For if we believe that Jesus died and rose again, so also we believe that God will bring with him those who have fallen asleep as Christians. (1 Thess. 4:14)

This verse contains an awkward "if-then" statement. Paul is not saying that *if* we do not believe Jesus died and rose again, *then* God will not cause souls to be brought back with Jesus. Instead, the sense of the condition is since we believe in the truth of the resurrection of Jesus, it *follows theologically* that we should also believe in the resurrection of believers. He teaches the Corinthian believers this same truth: "Now God indeed raised the Lord and he will raise us by his power" (1 Cor. 6:14; cf. 2 Cor. 4:14). At the return of Jesus, the Father will cause all the believing deceased, who exist as disembodied souls, to accompany Jesus from heaven. The destination from heaven to the sky will be made explicit in verses 16–17. The last statement in verse 14, "God will bring with him those who have fallen asleep as Christians," is developed in the next few verses.

Paul on the Resurrection and Rapture

> For we tell you this by the word of the Lord, that we who are alive, who are left until the coming of the Lord, will surely not go ahead of those who have fallen asleep. For the Lord himself will come down from heaven with a shout of command, with the voice of the archangel, and with the trumpet of God, and the dead in Christ will rise first. Then we who are alive, who are left, will be suddenly caught up together with them in the clouds to meet the Lord in the air. And so we will always be with the Lord. Therefore encourage one another with these words. (1 Thess. 4:15–18)

In verse 15, Paul begins to elaborate on God's initial purpose for the return of Jesus, the relationship between the soon-to-be-resurrected and the believers who are alive. Paul notes the source for his authoritative teaching: "by the word of the Lord." This "word" refers to the content in verses 16–18 (verse 15 is Paul's own anticipatory summary). In the Old Testament, the expression "word of the Lord" would have announced a prophetic oracle, but in the New Testament, this expression denotes the gospel itself or a teaching of Jesus during his ministry. In our passage, it is most certain that Paul is drawing from Jesus' Olivet Discourse because of the many parallels he uses.

The second part of verse 15 uses the phrase: "we who are alive, who are left until the coming of the Lord." Paul does not simply say "we who are *alive*," but rather clarifies it with "who are *left* until the coming of the Lord." He uses both of these phrases together again in verse 17. The Greek term is *hoi perileipomenoi* ("who are left"). When applied to humans, as it is here, it indicates survival. In addition, this term in biblical, Jewish, and secular usage can mean not just survival, but survival from some tragedy in which others have died.[21] Paul is likely using this term to allude to Jesus' teaching on the great tribulation. Incidentally, the term "asleep" in antiquity was used often as a euphemism for death, but Paul probably gives it a connotation for the future resurrection of believers.

In addition, Paul teaches that those who survive ("who are left *until* the coming of the Lord") live right up to the parousia. This shows there is no gap of time between the rapture and his coming; the rapture is an initial event of the parousia of Christ. Thus Paul envisions the last generation of the church surviving under very difficult circumstances right up to the parousia. In his second epistle, Paul again depicts hardship as normative for believers just before the Lord comes back.

> For it is right for God to repay with affliction those who afflict you, and to you who are being afflicted to give rest together with us when the Lord Jesus is revealed from heaven with his mighty angels. (2 Thess. 1:6–7)

This is consistent with my earlier discussion on how Jesus de-scribes a surviving remnant experiencing persecution right up to the time of his coming—persecution that will eventually be cut short by that coming (Matt. 24:15; 21–22; 29–31).

The last part of 1 Thessalonians 4:15 states that the living remnant of believers "will surely not go ahead of those who have fallen asleep." This implies that the Thessalonian defec-tive (i.e. uniformed) eschatology was the belief that those alive would be at an advantage at Christ's parousia. Paul, however, stresses that not only will the alive *not* go ahead of the dead in Christ, but the dead in Christ will receive glorified bodies *be-fore* those alive in Christ receive theirs. Accordingly, Paul gives comfort to the Thessalonians by teaching that their dead loved ones in Christ will participate at the parousia, even figuring prominently!

Let us take a step back and see where we are at this point in Paul's reasoning. In verse 13, Paul states the problem: The Thes-salonians are grieving hopelessly ("Now we do not want you to be uninformed, brothers and sisters, about those who are asleep, so that you will not grieve like the rest who have no hope"). In verse 14, he provides his main point for comfort ("we believe that God will bring with him those who have fallen asleep as Christians"). In verse 15, he begins to support the main point with a summary of the word of the Lord ("that we who are alive, who are left until the coming of the Lord, will surely not go ahead of those who have fallen asleep"). Now in verses 16–17, Paul gives us the word of the Lord elaborating on the main point:

> For the Lord himself will come down from heaven with a shout of command, with the voice of the archangel, and with the trumpet of God, and the dead in Christ will rise first. Then we who are alive, who are left, will be suddenly caught up to-gether with them in the clouds to meet the Lord in the air. And so we will always be with the Lord.

These two verses have given the church the popular rapture teaching, spawning many sermons, songs, and novels. My aim here is to give a careful interpretation of Paul's intention by not allowing the text to say more or less than it does.

First, the passage stresses that it is the Lord *himself* who will descend from heaven to the clouds. The Groom is personally coming for his bride. This is in fulfillment of the angelic prophecy at Christ's ascension in which it was said that he would come back to the sky with theophanic clouds (Acts 1:9–11).

Next, Paul teaches us there will be a triad of glorious, booming sounds accompanying Christ's descent: "with a *shout* of command, with the *voice* of the archangel, and with the *trumpet* of God" (emphasis mine). This will not be a "secret return" of Jesus! Some interpreters have seen this triad as a single sound described three different ways. But most have (rightly) interpreted this in a more natural way as three distinct sounds, with each serving a different function.

The first sound is a shouting command, which suggests that it will come from the Lord himself to "wake" the dead in Christ. During Jesus' earthly ministry he commanded a dead person to come alive in a similar way: "He shouted in a loud voice, 'Lazarus, come out!'" (John 11:43). Jesus' life-creating command foreshadows the macrocosmic resurrection of the saints. In the second sound, Paul notes "the voice of the archangel." We are not given the name of the archangel, and it is difficult to know what role this voice will have. Perhaps the voice will serve to give instructions to the hosts of angels to gather the saints since archangels rule over angels and a host of angels will come with Christ at his return (Matt. 24:31; 2 Thess. 1:7; Luke 9:26). The third sound is "the trumpet of God." Trumpet blasts served different purposes in ancient Israel. They were used for assemblies, warnings, battles, liturgies, and coronation ceremonies (e.g. Num. 10:2–10). An important trumpet of God sounded at Sinai (e.g. Exod. 19:16; 20:18). In our immediate context, the trumpet is related to the resurrection and gathering of all God's people.

We need to be particularly careful here since the Bible mentions different eschatological trumpets that will be blown. We should not be quick to assume that every trumpet blast is the same. The passage says it is the "trumpet of God," which emphasizes the possessive nature, giving it a decreeing action. There are two parallel passages having the same trumpet in view.

> "He will send his angels with a loud trumpet blast, and they will gather his elect from the four winds, from one end of heaven to the other." (Matt. 24:31)

Jesus calls it a "loud trumpet blast." We know that it is the same trumpet call as in 1 Thessalonians 4:16 because Jesus also teaches that it will be blown at his descent when the parousia begins, with both passages mentioning a universal gathering of God's people. The second parallel passage states,

> Listen, I will tell you a mystery: We will not all sleep, but we will all be changed—in a moment, in the blinking of an eye, at the last trumpet. For the trumpet will sound, and the dead will be raised imperishable, and we will be changed. (1 Cor. 15:51–52)

This passage is in the context of Paul's most descriptive treatment on the resurrection. After a discussion about the resurrection, he shifts his attention to those who will still be alive at Christ's parousia. He says his teaching is a "mystery." Paul does not mean it is a mystery in the sense of keeping his readers in the suspenseful dark. Quite the contrary. He is saying that this revelation has not been previously disclosed by God. What is this new revelation? Paul is teaching that God has ordained that the last generation of the church—those living up to the parousia—will not have to experience death ("we will not all sleep"). Just as the dead will be changed with imperishable, resurrected bodies, the living will also experience this change without having to die. Paul says this will happen at the "last trumpet," which will signal the resurrection and the transformation of those who are alive.[22]

The triad of glorious sounds announces God's parousia purposes. The first purpose is to "awaken" the dead in Christ. The newly resurrected are not caught up to the sky just yet, as we shall see in verse 17. God will apparently use the resurrected on earth as a testimony to the world to proclaim his power over death. This purpose will not be unprecedented, for God displayed his power similarly during his first coming at the death of Christ: "And tombs were opened, and the bodies of many saints who had died were raised. (They came out of the tombs after his resurrection and went into the holy city and appeared to many people)" (Matt. 27:52–53). At Christ's return, how long will the newly resurrected be on earth before the rapture? We are not told exactly, but the text suggests a brief period.

Next, verse 17 reads,

> Then we who are alive, who are left, will be suddenly caught up together with them in the clouds to meet the Lord in the air. And so we will always be with the Lord.

The dead in Christ will receive their new bodies first, followed by those who are alive and left at the parousia of Christ. Then at the same time both groups will be caught up in the clouds to meet the Lord in the air. Clouds are a common feature of theophanies accompanying divine presence. It is in those clouds that we meet and experience God's presence in his Son. It is often assumed that the alive will receive their new bodies *as they are being raptured* to the sky. But the text does not state this. Presumably, the alive in their newly transformed bodies will join with the newly resurrected *on earth* as a testimony to the world, then shortly after that union they will be raptured. It should not be assumed that the dead in Christ are raptured before the alive in Christ. The dead in Christ receive their transformed bodies before the alive receive theirs, but both groups—the resurrected and the remnant—will be united *together* on earth before they are raptured at the same time. Most translations indicate this picture, but the Greek text is explicit: *hama* ("together" or "at the same time") *syn* ("with") *autois* ("them") *harpagēsometha* ("snatched away"). Joseph Plevnik summarizes this depiction:

> The first act at the Lord's coming from heaven is that the deceased faithful are brought back to life; then only, once they have been reunited with the living, is everyone taken up by the clouds to meet the Lord. These pointers ["first," "then," "together with"] . . . insist on this sequence of acts. The surviving faithful have no advantage over the deceased: the latter are brought to life, join the living, and are, together with the living, taken up by the clouds.[23]

The Resurrection and the Rapture

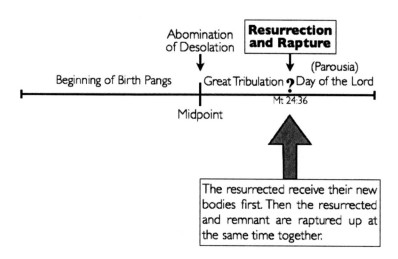

Harpazō—Snatching the Saints

I want to make a few comments on the Greek word *harpazō* that is behind the theological concept of the rapture. This word means "to snatch, take away, seize suddenly." It is the word used in verse 17 that underlies our English rendering "suddenly caught [up]."

This is where we get the concept of the rapture, which is a word derived from the Latin *rapio*. In the early church, one of the very first translations of the Bible was in Latin, and the translator chose *rapio* as the appropriate Latin verb to translate *harpazō*. Some have denied that the Bible teaches the rapture since the English term is not found in any English translations (even though the term "rapture" would be a very appropriate rendering for an English translation). This surface-level argument is not convincing since the concept of the rapture is clearly taught in verse 17. The lack of the term itself is not unusual because many English theological terms are not found in the Bible while their concepts are found therein. Examples include the Trinity, monotheism, inspiration, omniscience, and scores of others.

The term *harpazō* is found fourteen times in the New Testament.[24] (To be sure, the term is found in contexts other than the rapture.) Verse 17 is not the only place in the Bible where the concept occurs. There are six other biblical instances of a rapture:

1. Jesus raptured (*harpazō*) at his ascension (Rev. 12:5).
2. Paul raptured (*harpazō*) temporarily into heaven (2 Cor. 12:2, 4).
3. Philip raptured (*harpazō*) to Azotus (Acts 8:39–40, a "horizontal rapture").
4. The two witnesses will be raptured (*anabainō*) to heaven (Rev. 11:11–12). Though not using the term *harpazō*, another fitting word, *anabainō*, is used, meaning "to be in motion upward, go up, ascend."

We usually do not think of the Old Testament as containing examples of a rapture, but here are two instances:

5. Enoch was raptured (Gen. 5:24). The Hebrew term *lāqaḥ* in this verse means "to remove someone." In this context, Enoch was removed from the earth (cf. Heb. 11:5).[25]
6. Elijah was raptured (2 Kings 2:1). The Hebrew term *'lh* means "to cause to go up" (cf. 2 Kings 2:9–11).[26]

Where Do Believers Go after the Rapture?

The last part of verse 17 climaxes with reassurance: "And so we will always be with the Lord." Where will we spend eternity? In this passage, we are not told specifically. Paul's purpose is to stress that we will be *with* the Lord. But he does tell us that we will meet him in the clouds. From the clouds, where is our destination? Where will believers go after they are united with Christ in the sky? Do they remain in the air? Do they go straight to heaven forever? Do they immediately descend to the earth? Or is there another answer?

I believe we will be in fullness of fellowship and worship with our Lord *eventually* on earth. The locus of heaven will be the New Jerusalem, which will descend and establish itself on earth (see Revelation 21:1–22:5). But the question remains, where will the people of God dwell between the time of the rapture and the coalescing of the New Jerusalem on earth? There are four passages that give us the answer, revealing that the Lord will first escort his people temporarily to the heavenly abode (into the Father's presence) before we later make our descent to our eternal home on earth. Paul wrote of this time:

> We do so because we know that the one who raised up Jesus will also raise us up with Jesus and will bring us with you into his [Father's] presence (2 Cor. 4:14).

Before his departure Jesus promised,

> "There are many dwelling places in my Father's house. Otherwise, I would have told you, because I am going away to make ready a place for you. And if I go and make ready a place for you, I will come again and take you to be with me, so that where I am you may be too." (John 14:2–3)

Finally, the book of Revelation says,

> Then one of the elders asked me, "These dressed in long white robes—who are they and where have they come from?" So I said to him, "My lord, you know the answer." Then he said to me, "These are the ones who have come out of the great tribulation. They have washed their robes and made them white in the blood of the Lamb! For this reason they are before the throne of God, and they serve him day and night in his temple, and the one seated on the throne will shelter them." (Rev. 7:13–15)

There is a helpful fourth passage, although only implying that we are taken before the throne of the Father. Isaiah says,

> Your dead will come back to life; your corpses will rise up. Wake up and shout joyfully, you who live in the ground! For you will grow like plants drenched with the morning dew, and the earth will bring forth its dead spirits. Go, my people! Enter your inner rooms! Close your doors behind you! Hide for a little while, until his angry judgment is over! For look, the Lord is coming out of the place where he lives, to punish the sin of those who live on the earth. The earth will display the blood shed on it; it will no longer cover up its slain." (Isa. 26:19–21)

These passages picture the Lord escorting believers into the presence of the Father. The Lord then will mete out his eschatological wrath upon the ungodly on earth. But the church will not remain in heaven because the New Jerusalem will eventually descend to the earth for the millennium and eternity.

Destination of the Raptured

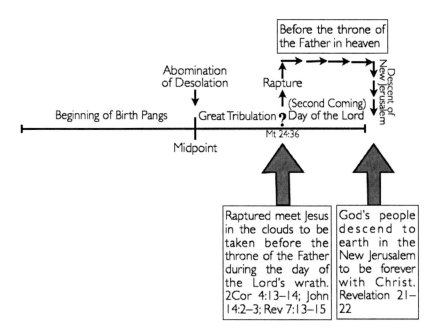

A Final Word on Biblical Hope

In verse 13, Paul exhorts the Thessalonians not to be hopelessly grieving. Similarly, he concludes with the exhortation: "Therefore encourage one another with these words" (1 Thess. 4:18). This encouragement transcends the local Thessalonian church to the universal church, which is why this passage is commonly read at funerals. But it can apply only to believers, for biblical hope is not the same as worldly hope. The world uses "hope" in the sense of probability, possibility, chance, or optimism. But biblical hope is certain. I once heard a Christian writer comment on biblical hope saying colloquially, "We can take it to the bank!" It is not simply Paul's words giving hope, for it is "the word of the Lord." And it is not a one-time exhortation because Paul says to encourage "one another," intending it to be a frequent reminder among members of the church, a mutual encouragement.

Christians possess biblical peace, which is based solely on God's promises, his faithfulness. The world does not—and cannot—offer such peace. Praise God that death is not the end of all things. This would be despair, no hope, no joy. Thankfully, our earthly peace is grounded in the reality that "we will always be with the Lord."

Four Reasons the Rapture Is in Matthew 24:31

Having examined in depth Paul's teaching on the resurrection and the rapture, this now brings us back to Jesus' teaching on the gathering of the elect.

> "And he will send his angels with a loud trumpet blast, and they will gather his elect from the four winds, from one end of heaven to the other." (Matt. 24:31)

Does the phrase "gather his elect" refer to the rapture? This is a watershed question. It is important because, if it does, then the church will face the Antichrist's great tribulation. Jesus ominously warns, "Remember, I have told you ahead of time" (Matt. 24:25). Jesus does not simply say, "Remember, I have told you"; he says, "Remember, I have told you *ahead of time.*" It is incumbent upon the student of prophecy to understand not just *that* Jesus is returning, but the *conditions* before his return, especially the event of the Antichrist's persecution. So this is a vital question for our study. We will consider four key reasons why Matthew 24:31 refers to the rapture.

The Gathering of the Elect as the Rapture

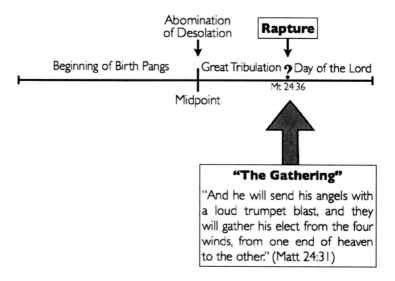

Reason 1: Jesus Uses 'Rapture' Language

A common objection to Matthew 24:31 containing a reference to the rapture is that Jesus never used rapture language in Matthew 24. This is a mistaken belief. In 2 Thessalonians 2:1, Paul writes,

> Now regarding the arrival of our Lord Jesus Christ and *our being gathered* [*episynagōgē*] to be with him, we ask you, brothers and sisters . . . (emphasis mine)

In this verse, even pretribulationists agree that Paul is referring to his rapture teaching in 1 Thessalonians 4:17 by using the term *episynagōgē*, meaning an "assembly or gathering." Why is Paul's use of this term significant? Because Jesus uses the same term in Matthew 24:31:

> "And he will send his angels with a loud trumpet blast, and they will gather [*episynagō*] his elect from the four winds, from one end of heaven to the other."

Jesus employs the action form of this same word, *episynagō*. To be sure, this is not a technical term for the rapture because it can be used in other contexts. However, the point is that it is fallacious and inconsistent to claim that Paul can use this term to refer to the rapture, but Jesus cannot. Paul's application of *episynagō* makes it baseless to claim that Jesus cannot use it in this same way, especially since Paul is drawing his teaching from Jesus! It makes perfect sense that, in referring to the rapture, Paul uses Jesus' own terminology (see the appendix, "Parallels between Jesus and Paul").

Besides *episynagō*, there is another "rapture" term Jesus uses in Matthew 24. Many pretribulationists claim that Jesus never taught the rapture before his resurrection; it was only after his resurrection that he began teaching this "church truth." This is deeply mistaken for several reasons. It is absurd to think that Jesus cannot introduce new revelation to his disciples (unrevealed in the Old Testament). His teaching ministry was all about new revelation! It is circular reasoning to essentially state, "Jesus did not teach the rapture before his resurrection because Jesus did not teach the rapture before his resurrection." Yet many of these same pretribulationists inconsistently agree that Jesus taught the rapture just three days after his Olivet Discourse in his Farewell Discourse, which was also given before his resurrection. They cannot have it both ways, asserting that Jesus never taught the rapture before his resurrection, while at the same time asserting that he did teach the rapture before the resurrection.

Here is the point: In Jesus' Farewell Discourse, John records a rapture teaching from Jesus.

> "Do not let your hearts be distressed. You believe in God; believe also in me. There are many dwelling places in my Father's house. Otherwise, I would have told you, because I am going away to make ready a place for you. And if I go and make ready a place for you, I will come again and take [*paralambanō*] you to be with me, so that where I am you may be too." (John 14:1–3)

Pretribulationists agree that the expression "take you to be with me" refers to the rapture. Prewrath theology agrees as well. So how does Jesus' teaching here relate to his Olivet Discourse? The Greek term behind "take" is *paralambanō*, which has a positive connotation often used in an intimate sense to take into close association, take to oneself, or take along. In Matthew 24:40–41, Jesus uses this same term in an agricultural illustration for the gathering of the elect at his parousia.

> "Then there will be two men in the field; one will be taken [*paralambanō*] and one left. There will be two women grinding grain with a mill; one will be taken [*paralambanō*] and one left."

This fact undermines the pretribulational claim that Jesus cannot be using rapture language in Matthew 24. It is inconsistent to hold that Jesus is allowed to use rapture language one day before his crucifixion in his Farewell Discourse but not allowed to use rapture language three days earlier in his Olivet Discourse![27]

Reason 2: Jesus' Use of Daniel on the Resurrection

In the previous point, I argued that Jesus uses "rapture" terminology in his Olivet Discourse, contrary to the claim by pretribulationists. Another objection pretribulationists put forward is the absence of any mention of a resurrection in Matthew 24. However, a closer look at Jesus' teaching in Matthew 24 shows that he is, in fact, referring to the resurrection. A passage does not have to explicitly use the word "resurrection" to refer to the resurrection. For example, pretribulationists agree that John 14:3 presupposes that the resurrection must occur before Jesus comes to receive his people, even though there is no mention of the resurrection itself: "And if I go and make ready a place for you, I will come again and take you to be with me, so that where I am you may be too." Likewise, in Matthew 24:31, the gathering of the elect relates to the resurrection. How do we know this to be the case?

The book of Daniel was the principle source on which Jesus drew for his Olivet Discourse: "So when you see the abomination of desolation—spoken about by Daniel the prophet—standing in the holy place . . . ." (Matt. 24:15). When we employ the principle of interpretation of comparing Scripture with Scripture, we discover that Jesus intends for the gathering in Matthew 24:31 to relate to the resurrection mentioned in the book of Daniel.

In support of this understanding, we see that Daniel 11:36–12:3 contains a sequence of four key events corresponding to the same sequence in Matthew 24, as the following juxtaposition illustrates:

Daniel 11:36–12:3 Parallels Matthew 24:15–31

The Abomination of Desolation

Daniel: Then the king will do as he pleases. He will exalt and magnify himself above every deity and he will utter presumptuous things against the God of gods. He will succeed until the time of wrath is completed, for what has been decreed must occur. . . . He will pitch his royal tents between the seas toward the beautiful holy mountain. But he will come to his end, with no one to help him (Dan. 11:36, 45).

Olivet Discourse: "So when you see the abomination of desolation—spoken about by Daniel the prophet—standing in the holy place" (Matt. 24:15).

The Great Tribulation

Daniel: There will be a time of distress unlike any other from the nation's beginning up to that time (Dan. 12:1).

Olivet Discourse: "For then there will be great suffering unlike anything that has happened from the beginning of the world until now, or ever will happen" (Matt. 24:21).

Rescue of Elect Remaining

Daniel: But at that time your own people, all those whose names are found written in the book, will escape (Dan. 12:1).
Olivet Discourse: "And if those days had not been cut short, no one would be saved [delivered]. But for the sake of the elect those days will be cut short" (Matt. 24:22).

Resurrection

Daniel: Many of those who sleep in the dusty ground will awake (Dan. 12:2).
Olivet Discourse: "They will gather his elect from the four winds, from one end of heaven to the other" (Matt. 24:31).

This last verse from Daniel 12:2 is considered to be the most explicit reference in the Old Testament to the resurrection: "those who sleep in the dusty ground will awake." Since Jesus explicitly says that he is citing Daniel, and since the sequence of these four events corresponds to Matthew 24, the natural conclusion is that Jesus intends those gathered "from the four winds, from one end of heaven to the other" to refer to the resurrection of God's people. When the disciples sitting on the Mount of Olives heard Jesus refer to the most explicit resurrection passage in the Old Testament, undoubtedly they would have associated "gather his elect" with the resurrection.

Reason 3: Jesus and Paul Address the Inception of the Parousia

Pretribulationists claim that Jesus and Paul are addressing two separate aspects of the parousia (i.e. a "two-stage" coming). They argue that Paul addresses the *inception* of the parousia as being a "secret, imminent" rapture, while Jesus focuses on the battle of Armageddon, with both stages separated by seven years. This pretribulational interpretation is mistaken. I will argue that the focus of both Jesus and Paul is on the same period of the parousia—the inception.

Inception of the Second Coming (Parousia)

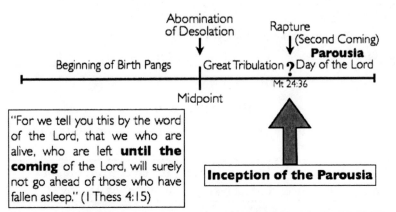

No one disagrees that Paul is expounding on the initial aspect of the parousia, teaching that the resurrection and rapture will happen immediately when Christ comes back. Paul writes,

> For we tell you this by the word of the Lord, that we who are alive, who are left *until* the coming of the Lord, will surely not go ahead of those who have fallen asleep. (1 Thess. 4:15, emphasis mine)

Notice that Paul states "until" the coming (*parousia*) of the Lord, which addresses the inception of the second coming of Christ. But what about Jesus? Does he also address the inception of the second coming? Or is he speaking of the battle of Armageddon? Jesus describes,

> "For just like the lightning comes from the east and flashes to the west, *so the coming [parousia] of the Son of Man will be.*

Wherever the corpse is, there the vultures will gather. Immediately after the suffering of those days, the sun will be darkened, and the moon will not give its light; the stars will fall from heaven, and the powers of heaven will be shaken. *Then the sign* of the Son of Man will appear in heaven, and all the tribes of the earth will mourn. They will see the Son of Man arriving on the clouds of heaven with power and great glory. And he will send his angels with a loud trumpet blast, and they will gather his elect from the four winds, from one end of heaven to the other." (Matt. 24:27–31, emphasis mine)

It is clear from this passage that Jesus is describing the inception of the parousia, not a later transpired stage.

First, Jesus gives the sign of the parousia (v. 27), which is the lightning, the Shekinah glory. He teaches that this bright sign will burst through when the natural light goes dark and the "powers of heaven are shaken" (vv. 30–31). It was the disciples' question that prompted this discourse: "Tell us, when will these things happen? And what will be the sign of your coming and of the end of the age?" (Matt. 24:3). Signs are given to announce something; thus, a sign for the inception of the parousia is precisely what Jesus gives in response to his disciples' question.

Second, Jesus' parables and similitudes explicitly address the inception of his return, not Armageddon (Matt. 24:32–51). His warnings to be watchful would be rendered unintelligible if applied to the end of the day of the Lord's wrath.

Third, Jesus states that the parousia will begin "immediately after" the great tribulation (v. 29). The persecution of God's people by the Antichrist will be cut short by the conjunction of the celestial disturbances and the sign of Christ's return, climaxing in the gathering of his elect.

Therefore, this notion that Paul and Jesus are teaching unrelated stages or aspects of the second coming is not supported by the biblical text. Instead, both are consistent in dealing with the beginning stage of the parousia. Jesus' mention of it is brief, while Paul elaborates on the event.[28]

Matthew 24:30 is Not Armageddon

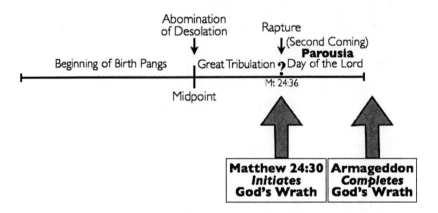

Reason 4: Gathered 'Out of the Great Tribulation'

We have seen that elements in Jesus' Olivet Discourse correspond sequentially to Revelation 6. This should not be surprising since Jesus is the source of both. There are seven seals on the scroll that must be opened before the contents of God's wrath are unleashed through the trumpets and bowls.

Revelation 6 describes six seals that open sequentially *without interruption*. But before the seventh seal is opened in Revelation 8:1, there is a conspicuous pause in Revelation 7. This interlude between the sixth and seventh seals depicts two groups of people being rescued: 144,000 Jews who are sealed on earth, protecting them from the impending wrath after the seventh seal is opened; and an innumerable crowd in heaven made up of believers from every nation, tribe, people, and language. Our attention will be on the innumerable crowd in heaven, but first I want to make a few comments about the 144,000 Jews on earth.

The Jewish Remnant Protected

After this I saw four angels standing at the four corners of the earth, holding back the four winds of the earth so no wind could blow on the earth, on the sea, or on any tree. Then I saw another angel ascending from the east, who had the seal of the living God. He shouted out with a loud voice to the four angels who had been given permission to damage the earth and the sea: "Do not damage the earth or the sea or the trees until we have put a seal on the foreheads of the servants of our God." Now I heard the number of those who were marked with the seal, one hundred and forty-four thousand, sealed from all the tribes of the people of Israel: From the tribe of Judah, twelve thousand were sealed, from the tribe of Reuben, twelve thousand, from the tribe of Gad, twelve thousand, from the tribe of Asher, twelve thousand, from the tribe of Naphtali, twelve thousand, from the tribe of Manasseh, twelve thousand, from the tribe of Simeon, twelve thousand, from the tribe of Levi, twelve thousand, from the tribe of Issachar, twelve thousand, from the tribe of Zebulun, twelve thousand, from the tribe of Joseph, twelve thousand, from the tribe of Benjamin, twelve thousand were sealed. (Rev. 7:1–8)

The first verse signals God's looming wrath: "four angels standing at the four corners of the earth holding back the four winds of the earth so no wind could blow on the earth, on the sea, or on any tree." The wording is strikingly similar to that of Jesus in his Olivet Discourse: "[His angels] will gather his elect from the four winds, from one end of heaven to the other" (Matt. 24:31). Before his wrath begins, God will sovereignly protect a group of 144,000 Jews by having them marked with his seal: "Do not damage the earth or the sea or the trees until we have put a seal on the foreheads of the servants of our God" (Rev. 7:3). This indicates that the day of the Lord's wrath has not yet begun. The sealing functions as protection from God's wrath.

Many interpreters identify the 144,000 as the church. The passage, however, explicitly identifies these 144,000 as Jews from specific tribes. It is mistaken to find some mysterious symbolism in this group and conclude that it is not speaking of literal Jews. This departs from a natural reading of the text. Therefore, without a deeper symbolic meaning for this passage, I interpret this in a face-value fashion.[29]

A final observation is the nature of these 144,000 Jews. Not only are they from the tribes of Israel, but they are also called "servants of our God." The term for servant is *doulos*, which in this spiritual context means to be a slave of God, solely committed and controlled by him to serve his purposes.

Pretribulationism has assumed the 144,000 to be Jewish "evangelists" who will cause a world revival. But their presupposition is problematic because there is no hint that the 144,000 Jews are evangelists. It is a faulty assumption based on their pretribulational system. Further, there is no evidence of a revival during the great tribulation or during the day of the Lord's wrath. To be sure, there will be a revival during the great tribulation in the sense of renewal for those who are *already* believers, the remnant. Persecution will strengthen and renew their faith and love for God. As far as Scripture indicating a world revival during the day of the Lord's wrath, I do not see this. Instead, we read that the ungodly will refuse to repent. This will be a time characterized by hardness of heart, idolatry, and wrath (Rev. 9:20, 21; 16:9, 11). To be sure, there will be a remnant of believing Jews and Gentiles who enter and populate the millennium (e.g. Romans 11; Matt. 25:31–46; Isaiah 56), but we should avoid thinking that unbelievers will be given a "second chance" during the day of the Lord. *Today* is the day of salvation. Any repentance by Gentiles and Jews during the day of the Lord's wrath will occur through God's gracious exception; it will not be the rule.

The Innumerable Multitude Raptured

> After these things I looked, and here was an enormous crowd that no one could count, made up of persons from every nation, tribe, people, and language, standing before the throne and before the Lamb dressed in long white robes, and with palm branches in their hands. They were shouting out in a loud voice, "Salvation belongs to our God, to the one seated on

the throne, and to the Lamb!" And all the angels stood there in a circle around the throne and around the elders and the four living creatures, and they threw themselves down with their faces to the ground before the throne and worshiped God, saying, "Amen! Praise and glory, and wisdom and thanksgiving, and honor and power and strength be to our God for ever and ever. Amen!" Then one of the elders asked me, "These dressed in long white robes—who are they and where have they come from?" So I said to him, "My lord, you know the answer." Then he said to me, "These are the ones who have come out of the great tribulation. They have washed their robes and made them white in the blood of the Lamb! For this reason they are before the throne of God, and they serve him day and night in his temple, and the one seated on the throne will shelter them. They will never go hungry or be thirsty again, and the sun will not beat down on them, nor any burning heat, because the Lamb in the middle of the throne will shepherd them and lead them to springs of living water, and God will wipe away every tear from their eyes." (Rev. 7:9–17)

In contrast to the first group, which is seen on earth, this group is pictured as having been delivered to heaven. John sees "an enormous crowd that no one could count, made up of persons from every nation, tribe, people, and language." They are depicted as possessing newly resurrected bodies and praising God for their deliverance and resurrection: "dressed in long white robes, and with palm branches in their hands" and having "washed their robes and made them white in the blood of the Lamb." Certainly, the fifth seal martyrs should also be viewed among God's people in this picture. "Each of them was given a long white robe and they were told to rest for a little longer" (Rev. 6:11). The description "every nation, tribe, people, and language" (7:9) and their robes being washed "white in the blood of the Lamb" (7:14) attests to the description of the church and all of God's people mentioned back in Revelation 5:9: "You are worthy to take the scroll and to open its seals because you were killed, and at the cost of your own blood you have purchased for God persons from every tribe, language, people, and nation" (cf. 5:10 with 1:5–6).[30]

This great multitude of believers appearing in heaven confounds John, prompting him to ask, "Who are they and where have they come from?" (Rev. 7:13; cf. Rev. 7:16–17). He is told, "These are the ones who have come out of the great tribulation." This parallels Jesus' teaching that the elect will be gathered out of the great tribulation at his return. "And if those days [the great tribulation] had not been cut short, no one would be saved. But for the sake of the elect those days will be cut short . . . . And he will send his angels with a loud trumpet blast, and they will gather his elect from the four winds, from one end of heaven to the other" (Matt. 24:22, 31; cf. vv. 29–30). This gathering of God's people is also found in Luke's account. "But when these things begin to happen, stand up and raise your heads, because your redemption is drawing near" (Luke 21:28).

This innumerable multitude can be none other than the resurrected and raptured people of God. It is perfectly fitting to see them taken out of the great tribulation with glorified bodies to heaven at this point because it happens just before the seventh seal is opened, triggering the day of the Lord's wrath (Rev. 8:1). God is faithful, promising believers that they will not have to experience his wrath (1 Thess. 5:9). If you are a child of God, you can have confidence in being included in this "enormous crowd that no one could count . . . standing before the throne and before the Lamb" (Rev. 7:9).

In addition, both accounts in the Olivet Discourse and Revelation 6–7 show that this gathering of God's people happens just after the celestial disturbances (Matt. 24:29–31; Luke 21:25–28; Rev. 6:12–17). In other words, we can say that the fifth seal promises wrath; the sixth seal portends wrath; an interlude in Revelation 7 protects from wrath; and the seventh seal pronounces wrath.

Progression towards God's Wrath	
Seal 5	Promises God's Wrath
Seal 6	Portends God's Wrath
Interlude	Protects from God's Wrath
Seal 7	Pronounces God's Wrath

The parallels between Matthew 24 and Revelation 6–7 are illustrated in the following table.

Matthew 24	Parallels	Revelation 6–7
4–5	The Antichrist / False christs	First Seal (6:1–2)
6–7	Wars	Second Seal (6:3–4)
7	Famine	Third Seal (6:5–6)
9, 21–22	Martyrdom (Great Tribulation)	Fourth Seal (6:7–8)
9, 21–22	Result of Martyrdom (Great Tribulation)	Fifth Seal (6:9–11)
29	Celestial Disturbances	Sixth Seal (6:12–17)
30–31	Raptured Saints	Interlude (7:9–17)
14, 30, 37–41	Day of the Lord's Wrath	Seventh Seal (Trumpets, Bowls)

I have given four reasons supporting Matthew 24:31 as referring to the rapture.[31] The same language describing Jesus' return is found, not just in Matthew 24, but in Paul's teaching in 2 Thessalonians 2:1 and in the Upper Room Discourse in John 14:1–3. Jesus also draws from Daniel, especially from the most explicit resurrection passage in the Old Testament. In addition, the focus of both Jesus and Paul is on the inception of the second coming. The final reason I gave shows that Jesus and the book of Revelation address the same context and the same sequence of God's people who have "come out of the great tribulation." In my judgment, each reason is compelling, and collectively, they form a cogent defense.

In the second half of his teaching on his second coming in his Olivet Discourse, Jesus begins to warn against date-setting.

> "Learn this parable from the fig tree: Whenever its branch becomes tender and puts out its leaves, you know that summer is near. So also you, when you see all these things, know that he is near, right at the door. I tell you the truth, this generation will not pass away until all these things take place. Heaven and earth will pass away, but my words will never pass away. But as for that day and hour no one knows it—not even the angels in heaven—except the Father alone." (Matt. 24:32–36)

In the clearest of words, Jesus says we can be confident that we will know the season of his return "when you see all these things." Only when these conditions are met will Jesus be "near, right at the door." We will, however, not know the day or the hour. Date-setting is a futile exercise. *Hence, we should be content that we will know only the season.*

The remaining teaching in the Olivet Discourse exhorts believers to spiritual vigilance in light of Christ's delayed coming, lest he come back during a time in our lives when we are complacent. Jesus uses similes and parables to illustrate the need for spiritual watchfulness (Matt. 24:32–25:30). The Discourse concludes with a description of the Sheep-Goats Judgment (25:31–46).

Conclusion

In Part 2, I covered the unique cluster of celestial events that will warn the world of God's impending wrath, as well as be a signal to the church of their impending deliverance as they suffer during the Antichrist's persecution. Then I considered the teachings on the rapture, concluding with four reasons that the gathering in Matthew 24:31 refers to the rapture. In Part 3, we will consider the next event after the rapture—the day of the Lord's wrath. We will survey the day of the Lord that Jesus knew from selected Old Testament prophets and Paul's important teaching on God's eschatological wrath. I will conclude with the graphic portrayal of the day of the Lord's judgment from the book of Revelation.

An Overview of the Prewrath Position

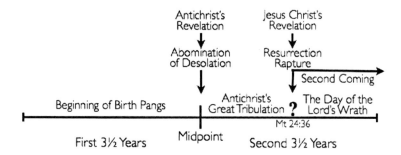

Part 3.
The Day of the Lord's Wrath

Part 3.
The Day of the Lord's Wrath

In our third and final part, I will describe the day of the Lord's wrath. It will be the eschatological period of judgment—fiery, dreadful, inescapable, bloody, and destructive. In short, Yahweh's judgment will be decisive. I will first consider the meaning of biblical theophanies and the expression "the day of the Lord." Then I will expound on the day of the Lord that Jesus knew from the Jewish prophets of old. After that, I will concentrate on Paul's main teaching on the day of the Lord, concluding with the book of Revelation's portrayal of the trumpet judgments, bowl judgments, and Armageddon.

Theophanies

Throughout history God has revealed himself through creation, the Spirit, angels, prophets, dreams, visions, consciences, and ultimately the incarnate Son of God, Jesus. God is sovereign, and when he desires to communicate his will, he can use any means, even a donkey (Num. 22:21–35). But one day there will be a divine revelation in which our Lord appears in the clouds to bestow glorified bodies and deliver his people. That day will be a joyous manifestation for those who belong to God, but a horrific, heart-stopping judgment for those who do not.

In the garden of Eden, Adam and Eve were the first humans to witness God's judgment. He graciously offered them paradise and intimate fellowship, but their faithfulness did not last. Our primal parents sinned. Soon after Adam and Eve sinned by eating from the tree of the knowledge of good and evil, God is said to have been "walking in the garden in the cool of the day." This portrayal seems to convey that God was cavalierly taking a stroll even while he knew our first parents had just sinned, bringing down all humanity. Didn't God tell Adam he would "surely die" if he disobeyed?

In recent decades, a growing number of Old Testament scholars have looked more closely at this text, concluding that the translation "walking in the garden in the cool of the day" is not the best rendering. The New English Translation contains a similar expression, "moving about in the orchard at the breezy time." Most traditional translations also render it as such; for example, "They heard the sound of the Lord God walking in the garden in the cool of the day, and the man and his wife hid themselves from the presence of the Lord God among the trees of the garden" (Gen. 3:8 NASB). However, the traditional rendering is not likely the best choice because of the judgment context. We have gained new understanding of this passage based on insights from ancient Near Eastern languages. A better rendering would be "shekinah-judgment of the day" or "in the wind of the storm."[32] These renderings seem to make better sense because this Genesis passage is found in the genre of a *judgment oracle*, consisting of elements such as breaking God's commands, the sound of the Lord God approaching, the shameful disobedient fleeing and hiding from God, and the Lord consequently pronouncing punishment on them.

This is what theologians call a *theophany*, and in this case, a judgment theophany. Theophanies (from the Greek compound for "god" and "to appear") are events in the Bible portraying God manifesting himself visually or audibly. A theophany does not mean someone is able to see God's spirit or essential being; they cannot (1 John 4:12). Rather, theophanies are supernatural occurrences such as the Shekinah (the glory of the divine presence), an angel of the Lord, or his spoken words. Theophanies reveal *and* conceal. God has revealed his glory in brightness like lightning and often concealed it through darkened clouds. If God were to reveal his whole self, any person would immediately perish from exposure to his pure holiness (Exod. 33:20). Accordingly, in his book on biblical theophanies, Jeffrey J. Niehaus offers this translation of the Genesis verse, bringing out the theophanic elements.

> Then the man and his wife heard the thunder of Yahweh God going back and forth in the garden in the wind of the storm, and they hid from Yahweh God among the trees of the garden. (Gen. 3:8)

Niehaus remarks, "Such was the first Sinai-like theophany—the first storm theophany when God appeared as Judge of his guilty people."[33] The New English Translation also comments on this verse in a note, stating that if this theophanic judgment rendering is correct, then:

> God is not pictured as taking an afternoon stroll through the orchard, but as coming in a powerful windstorm to confront the man and woman with their rebellion. In this case ["sound of the Lord"] may refer to God's thunderous roar, which typically accompanies his appearance in the storm to do battle or render judgment (cf. Ps. 29).

What does this have to do with the day of the Lord? God's judgment of Adam and Eve in the garden is a prototypical day of the Lord, giving us context for later theophanic episodes. One noted theologian has coined this microcosmic event as the "primal parousia" (first presence).[34] Considering this prototypical day of the Lord, we can begin to appreciate a biblical continuity of God's theophanic program, a continuity reaching all the way back to the garden and one day fully manifesting on the global-eschatological scale.

'Bookend' Theophanies

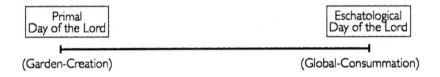

A parallel is also found between the human sin condition of our first parents desiring to be autonomous from God and the sin condition of the autonomy-seeking nations that will rebel at the eschatological-global theophany during the Lord's second coming. The apostle Paul recognized this condition when he wrote, "So then, just as sin entered the world through one man and death through sin, and so death spread to all people because all sinned" (Rom. 5:12). He describes how this fundamental sin culminates: "They exchanged the truth of God for a lie and worshiped and served the creation rather than the Creator" (Rom. 1:25). How do we escape from this human condition of sin and its eternal consequences? There is only one gospel of hope for deliverance from sin and "the coming wrath" (1 Thess. 1:10). That is the hope of justification, forgiveness, and peace with the Creator (Rom. 5:1). We have to turn away from our sin and place our trust in God's provision found only in the sacrificial death of Jesus on the cross, which removes the punishment of sin we deserve and reckons us as righteous before our holy Creator (Eph. 1–2).

Theophanies are found not only in the garden of Eden and at the return of Christ, but are dotted throughout the Bible. Indeed, while the return of the Lord will be the par excellence of theophanies (Matt. 24:30; 1 Thess. 4:16; 2 Thess. 1:7; Titus 2:13; Rev. 1:7), here is a sampling of other theophanies that have occurred at decisive moments in Israel's redemptive history: Jacob wrestling with God (Gen. 32:22–32), Moses at the burning bush (Exodus 3), the Exodus (Exod. 13:21–22), God at Sinai (Exodus 19), the news of the birth of Samson (Judges 13), and vividly calling prophets to ministry (Isaiah 6; Ezekiel 1). Angels and figures in human form have also manifested in biblical history, and it is correct to understand that many of these instances have been pre-incarnate appearances of Christ (technically, called "christophanies").[35] The New Testament is likewise punctuated with theophanies at key redemptive moments: the unique and ultimate theophany of Jesus' incarnation (John 1:14), Jesus' baptism (Mark 1:9–11), the Transfiguration (Matt. 17:1–8), Paul's conversion (Acts 9), Pentecost (Acts 2), and God's dwelling in Zion with his people for eternity (Isa. 2:3; Joel 3:17; Zech. 14:16–21; Rev. 21:1–4).

These theophanies reflect God's redemptive purpose to dwell with his people. Perhaps this is the central, unifying theological principle in the Bible. At creation we see God seeking fellowship with Adam and Eve; subsequently, the Old Testament story is God graciously seeking to dwell with his people Israel in the tabernacle and temple. In the New Testament God comes in the flesh to dwell: "Now the Word [Jesus] became flesh [took on humanity] and took up residence among us [to dwell with his people]" (John 1:14). In the church age, Jesus has sent the Holy Spirit to dwell with his people (John 16:7). And climactically, God's dwelling-purpose is immediately heralded at the end of the book of Revelation when the theophanic New Jerusalem descends.

> And I heard a loud voice from the throne saying: "Look! The residence of God is among human beings. He will live among them, and they will be his people, and God himself will be with them." (Rev. 21:3)

In the Bible, the consistent picture of God seeking to dwell with his people should give us peace, for God is not aloof in our trials, temptations, and fears. He is for us. He loves us and will dwell with us perfectly one day.

From Garden to Global
GENESIS-GARDEN
Paradise
Fellowship Broken
Primal Day of the Lord
Temporary Garments
REVELATION-GLOBAL
Eternal Garments
Eschatological Day of the Lord
Fellowship Renewed
Paradise Recreated

The Expression 'the Day of the Lord'

Some explanations will acquaint us with the terminology and concept of the day of the Lord. The personal name for God is Yahweh (YHWH), which is the Hebrew behind the word "Lord" in the expression "the day of the Lord." Many English translations render it with small capital letters (LORD), not to give emphasis, but to distinguish God's name from the regular lowercase "Lord," which is the Hebrew term *adonai*. The latter term usually refers to deity or a respectful address. I am keeping it simple. When I use the Old Testament expression "the day of the Lord," you can assume "Lord" is referring to God's name, Yahweh.

The Hebrew term for "day" in this expression is *yôm*. In our context, the term takes on a richer and larger scope than a mere literal twenty-four-hour day. *Yôm* contains about a dozen different meanings in the Old Testament, so context plays an important role. It does refer to a literal twenty-four-hour day when it is associated with a number (e.g. "three days") or other qualifiers such as "full day," "each day," "every day," "a full day," "the Sabbath day," and so on. In contrast, the prophets often used "day" to denote the epochal time when God would break into history in glory and judgment, bringing the ungodly to account. They describe this eschatological period as decisive, yet complex, unfolding over time. The book of Revelation reveals that the fifth trumpet judgment alone will last five months (Rev. 9:5, 10) and the seventh trumpet will unfold for an indeterminate number of days (Rev. 10:7).

The "day of the Lord" is not the only biblical expression to refer to God's eschatological judgment upon the ungodly. The Old and New Testaments use about twenty similar expressions.[36]

- the day of the Lord's sacrifice (Zeph. 1:8)
- the day of the Lord's wrath (Zeph. 1:18)
- in those days (Joel 3:1)
- the day (1 Thess. 5:4)
- the great Day (Jude 6)
- that day (Isa. 2:11)
- judgment day (Isa. 10:3)
- the day of his burning anger (Isa. 13:13)
- the day of vengeance (Isa. 34:8)
- a day is coming for the Lord (Zech. 14:1)
- unique day (Zech. 14:7)
- the harvest (Matt. 13:39)
- the coming of the Son of Man (Matt. 24:37)
- the days of the Son of Man (Luke 17:26)
- the day of wrath (Rom. 2:5)
- the day of Christ (Phil. 1:10)
- the last day (John 12:48)
- the day of judgment (2 Pet. 2:9)
- the day of God (2 Pet. 3:12)
- the great day of God (Rev. 16:14)

Thus we have to be careful not to narrowly think that if a passage does not contain the exact expression "day of the Lord," it cannot apply to the concept of God's eschatological judgment.[37] As seen above, the biblical prophets and writers had the flexibility of literary expression. For consistency, however, I have mostly used the expression "day of the Lord," while recognizing that the Bible employs diverse expressions. These expressions may denote the complete day of the Lord or some stage within it, such as the inception, consummation, or other elements, depending on their respective contexts. In other words, every passage on the day of the Lord contributes to the larger picture. For instance, Joel 2:30–31 and Revelation 6:17 use expressions focusing on the *impending* wrath of God, while Revelation 16:14 contains an expression drawing attention to the later *climactic* judgment, the battle of Armageddon.

There are a couple of other notions about the day of the Lord that require brief qualification. My purpose is to describe a biblical picture of eschatological judgment; however, we need to be aware that the biblical prophets could also speak of a historical day of the Lord's judgment in their own times (e.g. Joel 1:15; 2:1, 11; Amos 5:18; Ezek. 13:5; Lam. 1:12; 2:1). The most noted historical day of the Lord judgments were the downfall of the northern kingdom in 722 B.C., the end of Nineveh in 612 B.C., the fall of Jerusalem and Judah of the southern kingdom in 586 B.C., and the end of the Babylonian Empire in 538 B.C. The prophets often used these judgments as a pattern or foreshadowing for the larger-in-scope eschatological judgment, urging the people to repent of their idolatry and trust in their covenantal God.

In prophetic literature, there is also the phenomenon called "foreshortening" or "telescoping." A prophet could speak of two events successively, with the events appearing to be fulfilled in conjunction with each other, while the contextual indicators and future revelation in the New Testament reveal that the events are actually fulfilled in separate epochs. For example, we will see below that the prophet Joel describes a catastrophic day-of-the-Lord judgment in his own time; yet immediately following his portrayal, he draws from this language to point to the eschatological day of the Lord.

Just as there are day-of-the-Lord judgments that have intruded into Old Testament history and anticipate the final eschatological "day," New Testament saints live in a similar tension. During

Jesus' ministry, we find a day-of-the-Lord judgment, not upon any group of people, but in the climactic death of Christ on the cross where he absorbed the wrath of God in the place of sinners. This "day of the Lord" did not usher in the complete new creation, fulfilling all things, but we do live in faith that the new creation will be completed one day. The blood of Christ shed on the cross delivers the church from experiencing the eschatological wrath; while the ungodly during that day will experience God's wrath, shedding their own blood for their own sin.

In short, we can say that Jesus suffered a day of the Lord on behalf of his people during his first coming so we will not be required to suffer the day of the Lord during his second coming. In the larger scope of eternal punishment, Jesus lovingly absorbed the wrath of God on the cross so his people would not have to endure eternal perdition. That is the gospel: Someone must pay the penalty for our sin. Was it paid on the cross *by* Christ? Or will you pay it eternally apart *from* Christ? There is no third option. God's holiness and righteousness must be satisfied and upheld.

There are some elements associated with the crucifixion judgment that serve as a pattern for the future eschatological judgment when Christ returns.

Day of the Lord Imagery in the Crucifixion
God's Wrath Expressed upon His Son (Isa. 53:5)
Resurrection (Matt. 27:52–53)
Earthquake (Matt. 27:54)
Sun's Light Failed and Darkness (Luke 23:44–45)

All of this judgment discussion about the day of the Lord can give the impression that judgment will be the only characteristic of this day. The same prophets who spoke of eschatological judgment upon the ungodly, however, also prophesied that this "day" would encompass future hope, redemption, and millennial blessings for the righteous (e.g. Isaiah 27, 40–66; Mic. 4:6–8; Obadiah 15–17; Jer. 30:8–9; Zeph. 3:9–20; Zechariah 14). My emphasis on the judgment aspect of this "day" for prewrath purposes is not meant to minimize the importance of the millennial blessings and God's glorious goal to dwell with his people. For that, I direct the reader elsewhere to helpful literature concentrating on the day-of-the-Lord blessings in the millennial kingdom.[38]

Types of Day of the Lord

```
                    Historical              Eschatological
                    Day of the Lord         Day of the Lord
        Primal                   Crucifixion                Millennial
   Day of the Lord               Day of the Lord           Day of the Lord
   |————————————————————————————————————————————————————————|
```

The Day of the Lord That Jesus Knew

It should go without saying that there was no "New Testament" during the time of Jesus. The Scriptures that Jesus knew were the Hebrew Scriptures (the "Old Testament"), also called the Jewish Bible (Tanakh).[39] The Jewish prophets of old that Jesus knew depicted a vivid picture of God's eschatological wrath.

The prophets were privileged ministers who extolled God's holy and faithful attributes, calling Israel back to covenant faithfulness. When Israel did not repent, God vindicated his holiness by judging the rebellious nation. The prophets repeatedly reminded the Israelites of the choice between God's kingdom and human kingdoms—the former characterizing obedience, the latter obstinacy. The prophets pointed to the eventual defeat of human kingdoms to be replaced by the kingdom of peace where God's people would fellowship forever with their Covenant-Creator. But before the kingdom of peace is recreated, the human kingdoms will be purged by God's wrath. This is the consistent message of the prophets, who provide us with a poignant picture. We will look at five of these prophets—Joel, Isaiah, Obadiah, Zephaniah, and Amos—who will help us paint this picture of Yahweh's eschatological wrath.

Joel on the Day of the Lord's Wrath

The Bible gives minimal biographical information about this prophet. But it is suggested that he was from the southern kingdom of Judah, possibly even Jerusalem. The chief message in the book of Joel is the day of the Lord, both historical and eschatological. In Joel 1–2:11, a contemporaneous locust plague had invaded Israel, which Joel used to prefigure the near invasion by the Assyrians and Babylonians. He also used it to foreshadow the unparalleled eschatological day of the Lord (2:28–3:21). In response, Joel calls Israel to return to the Lord by repenting of the people's neglect of the law of God (2:12–27). The sober and vivid theophanic imagery speaks for itself.

> Blow the trumpet in Zion; sound the alarm signal on my holy mountain! Let all the inhabitants of the land shake with fear, for the day of the Lord is about to come. Indeed, it is near! It will be a day of dreadful darkness, a day of foreboding storm clouds, like blackness spread over the mountains. It is a huge and powerful army—there has never been anything like it ever before, and there will not be anything like it for many generations to come! Like fire they devour everything in their path; a flame blazes behind them. The land looks like the Garden of Eden before them, but behind them there is only a desolate wilderness—for nothing escapes them! They look like horses; they charge ahead like war horses. They sound like chariots rumbling over mountain tops, like the crackling of blazing fire consuming stubble, like the noise of a mighty army being drawn up for battle. People writhe in fear when they see them. All of their faces turn pale with fright. They charge like warriors; they scale walls like soldiers. Each one proceeds on his course; they do not alter their path. They do not jostle one another; each of them marches straight ahead. They burst through the city defenses and do not break ranks. They rush into the city; they scale its walls. They climb up into the houses; they go in through the windows like a thief. The

earth quakes before them; the sky reverberates. The sun and the moon grow dark; the stars refuse to shine. The voice of the Lord thunders as he leads his army. Indeed, his warriors are innumerable; surely his command is carried out! Yes, the day of the Lord is awesome and very terrifying—who can survive it? (Joel 2:1–11)

Yet the prophet holds out hope, urging heart-contrite repentance.

Yet even now, the Lord says, "Return to me with all your heart—with fasting, weeping, and mourning. Tear your hearts, not just your garments!" Return to the Lord your God, for he is merciful and compassionate, slow to anger and boundless in loyal love—often relenting from calamitous punishment. (Joel 2:12–13)

We have already covered Joel's celestial disturbance passage in Part 2, but for completeness' sake, I will mention it again.

I will produce portents both in the sky and on the earth—blood, fire, and columns of smoke. The sunlight will be turned to darkness and the moon to the color of blood, before the day of the Lord comes—that great and terrible day! (Joel 2:30–31; cf. 3:14–15)

Finally, Joel teaches that the stormy wrath of the day of the Lord will not be limited to unrepentant Israel. The godless nations will endure fiery judgment, as well. This judgment is described in graphic agricultural imagery.

For look! In those days and at that time I will return the exiles to Judah and Jerusalem. Then I will gather all the nations, and bring them down to the valley of Jehoshaphat. I will enter into judgment against them there concerning my people Israel who are my inheritance, whom they scattered among the nations. They partitioned my land. . . . Let the nations be roused and let them go up to the valley of Jehoshaphat, for there I will sit in judgment on all the surrounding nations. Rush forth with the sickle, for the harvest is ripe! Come, stomp the grapes, for the winepress is full! The vats overflow. Indeed, their evil is great! Crowds, great crowds are in the valley of decision, for the day of the Lord is near in the valley of decision! The sun and moon are darkened; the stars withhold their brightness. The Lord roars from Zion; from Jerusalem his voice bellows out. The heavens and the earth shake. But the Lord is a refuge for his people; he is a stronghold for the citizens of Israel. (Joel 3:1–2, 12–16)

The book of Joel closes with the prophecy of the establishment of God's kingdom, the ultimate goal of the day of the Lord (3:17–21). The Lord shall reign and dwell in Zion.

To recap, Joel's description of the day of the Lord reveals it to be characterized by the following:

- Ominous celestial signs
- Dreadful darkness
- Fear and trembling
- Divine decisive judgment
- Presence of a powerful and numerous divine army
- Unprecedented terror
- Fire devouring everything in its path
- Unexpected calamity
- Limited survival

Isaiah on the Day of the Lord's Wrath

Isaiah prophesied during precarious days in the southern kingdom of Judah. His major themes, to name a few, include picturing the Lord as a warrior, redeemer, and a holy sovereign. He warned of impending judgment if the people did not turn back to God in faith and obedience. Here is one of his evocative pronouncements.

Go up into the rocky cliffs, hide in the ground. Get away from the dreadful judgment of the Lord, from his royal splendor! Proud men will be brought low, arrogant men will be humiliated; the Lord alone will be exalted in that day. Indeed, the Lord who commands armies has planned a day of judgment, for all the high and mighty, for all who are proud—they will be humiliated; for all the cedars of Lebanon, that are so high and mighty, for all the oaks of Bashan; for all the tall mountains, for all the high hills, for every high tower, for every fortified wall, for all the large ships, for all the impressive ships. Proud men will be humiliated, arrogant men will be brought low; the Lord alone will be exalted in that day. The worthless idols will be completely eliminated. They will go into caves in the rocky cliffs and into holes in the ground, trying to escape the dreadful judgment of the Lord and his royal splendor, when he rises up to terrify the earth. At that time men will throw their silver and gold idols, which they made for themselves to worship, into the caves where rodents and bats live, so they themselves can go into the crevices of the rocky cliffs and the openings under the rocky overhangs, trying to escape the dreadful judgment of the Lord and his royal splendor, when he rises up to terrify the earth. Stop trusting in human beings, whose life's breath is in their nostrils. For why should they be given special consideration? (Isa. 2:10–22)

This passage shows that, in that day, the ungodly will not repent when they see the Lord's royal splendor. Instead, they will run from him. This kind of fear does not lead to wisdom. It exposes foolish idolatry. The Lord alone will be exalted in that day, resulting in human humiliation. The world's so-called greatest achievements will no longer be celebrated. The Lord will demolish the eschatological towers of Babel, bringing them to their prideful knees. Self-exalting individuals who worship power, money, entertainment, and other idols will be "brought low." The response from the ungodly contrasts with Isaiah's response to witnessing the Lord's glory a few chapters later when he was given the rare privilege of seeing the Lord in splendid glory in his magnificent throne room. In chapter 6, he describes seeing the Lord of hosts as the seraphim solemnly praise, "Holy, holy, holy is the Lord." Isaiah recognizes his unworthiness and repents of his creaturely sin to purify himself for his prophetic ministry.

In this next passage, Isaiah portrays the ominous countenance of the ungodly.

> Wail, for the Lord's day of judgment is near; it comes with all the destructive power of the sovereign judge. For this reason all hands hang limp, every human heart loses its courage. They panic—cramps and pain seize hold of them like those of a woman who is straining to give birth. They look at one another in astonishment; their faces are flushed red. Look, the Lord's day of judgment is coming; it is a day of cruelty and savage, raging anger, destroying the earth and annihilating its sinners. Indeed the stars in the sky and their constellations no longer give out their light; the sun is darkened as soon as it rises, and the moon does not shine. I will punish the world for its evil, and wicked people for their sin. I will put an end to the pride of the insolent, I will bring down the arrogance of tyrants. I will make human beings more scarce than pure gold, and people more scarce than gold from Ophir. So I will shake the heavens, and the earth will shake loose from its foundation, because of the fury of the Lord who commands armies, in the day he vents his raging anger. (Isa. 13:6–13)

This passage applies to the near judgment on Judah by the Babylonians in 605–586 B.C. (see 13:1); but it also foreshadows the eschatological theophany. Isaiah 13 is a good example of how the prophets often blended the historical with the eschatological. They typically did not demarcate the eschatological with clear temporal indicators, so we have to look to other elements to give us clues. In chapter 13, within this oracle of Babylon, we can discern that parts of it refer to the larger eschatological judgment because of the universal terminology, such as "earth" and "world." In addition, the celestial portents in this passage are strikingly similar to other passages that are clearly in their own eschatological contexts (cf. Joel 2:30–31; Matt. 24:29; Rev. 6:12–13). This passage depicts a holy war compounded by universal catastrophe, a unilateral campaign by the Sovereign Warrior. It will be unabated wrath, resulting in terrified sinners and their destruction. Survival will be "more scarce than pure gold."

Similarly, Isaiah draws from Joel's motif of the celestial disturbances associated with the day of the Lord. There is not only a literal fulfillment in temporal darkness, but there is symbolism in this prophecy, as well. The concept of darkness is fitting since many pagan gods were identified with celestial bodies that give off light, including the moon, stars, and sun. Even today, naturalistic materialism holds that celestial bodies are an end unto themselves, coming into existence, not through a Creator, but through their own self-sustaining power. Accordingly, it will be ironic when God darkens the luminaries to display his own sovereign radiance (cf. Rom. 1:18–32).

The certainty of this day should induce us to examine ourselves for any worldly attachments fettering us from surrendering completely to the Lord of the universe. We should never be too confident, always asking God to search our souls for sin. For further reading on Isaiah's prophecies concerning God's future judgment and triumph over the earth, I refer the reader to Isaiah 24–27, which has been coined Isaiah's "Little Apocalypse."

To recap, Isaiah highlights these elements of the day of the Lord:

- The proud brought low in humiliation
- The ungodly attempting to flee from his judgment
- The Lord alone exalted
- False value of idols exposed
- Foolishness of trusting in human structures
- Utter terror and despair
- God's unabated fury

- Sinners punished
- Celestial darkness
- Unlikely survival

Obadiah on the Day of the Lord's Wrath

Obadiah is the shortest book in the Old Testament. Short books pack a powerful punch, often highlighting a single concern. Obadiah is no exception, giving a grave warning to the nations about God's eschatological judgment.

> For the day of the Lord is approaching for all the nations! Just as you have done, so it will be done to you. You will get exactly what your deeds deserve. (Obad. 1:15)

Obadiah reminds Edom that, because of its antagonistic treatment of its neighbor Israel (which is also its ancestral brother, Jacob), it will be recompensed. Obadiah teaches us that injustice can run, but it cannot hide—there will be divine justice. Wrongdoing against God's people requires divine reckoning. Obadiah encapsulates his primary message in this single verse: "Just as you have done, so it will be done to you. You will get exactly what your deeds deserve." Obadiah does not end on that note. God has promised to establish his kingdom, and Israel will be given new life. But God's kingdom will not be limited to Israel alone. It will be international in scope (vv. 16–21).

To recap, Obadiah teaches:

- Recompense from the nations
- Vindication for a holy God and his people
- Kingdom blessings

Zephaniah on the Day of the Lord's Wrath

This next prophet furnishes us with a compact yet vivid declaration of the day of the Lord. Zephaniah prophesied to Judah in the seventh century B.C., condemning salient sins such as pagan practices, idolatry, laziness, and pride. Soberly read his portrayal of the day of the Lord as God revealed it to him.

> This is the prophetic message that the Lord gave to Zephaniah son of Cushi, son of Gedaliah, son of Amariah, son of Hezekiah. Zephaniah delivered this message during the reign of King Josiah son of Amon of Judah: "I will destroy everything from the face of the earth," says the Lord. "I will destroy people and animals; I will destroy the birds in the sky and the fish in the sea. (The idolatrous images of these creatures will be destroyed along with evil people.) I will remove humanity from the face of the earth," says the Lord. . . . The Lord's great day of judgment is almost here; it is approaching very rapidly! There will be a bitter sound on the Lord's day of judgment; at that time warriors will cry out in battle. That day will be a day of God's anger, a day of distress and hardship, a day of devastation and ruin, a day of darkness and gloom, a day of clouds and dark skies, a day of trumpet blasts and battle cries. Judgment will fall on the fortified cities and the high corner towers. I will bring distress on the people and they will stumble like blind men, for they have sinned against the Lord. Their blood will be poured out like dirt; their flesh will be scattered like manure. Neither their silver nor their gold will be able to deliver them in the day of the Lord's angry judgment. The whole earth will be consumed by his fiery wrath. Indeed, he will bring terrifying destruction on all who live on the earth. (Zeph. 1:1–3, 14–18)

More than all the other prophets, Zephaniah highlights the universality of God's judgment. "'I will destroy everything from the face of the earth,' says the Lord" (1:2; cf. 3:8). Yahweh is not some mere tribal deity. He rules globally. Zephaniah characterizes this time as fiery wrath, devastation, darkness, and bloodshed for both beasts and humans. The Divine Warrior intrudes definitively into human history. The ungodly have no choice but to submit to his sovereign will. One author describes Zephaniah's eschatological intervention as the "divine-human collision."[40] Material investments will be impotent to deliver the rebellious in the day of the Lord's angry judgment.

In view of this dreadful picture of wrath, Zephaniah urges repentance and fervent devotion to the Lord.

> Before God's decree becomes reality and the day of opportunity disappears like windblown chaff, before the Lord's raging anger overtakes you—before the day of the Lord's angry judgment overtakes you! Seek the Lord's favor, all you humble people of the land who have obeyed his commands! Strive to do what is right! Strive to be humble! Maybe you will be protected on the day of the Lord's angry judgment. (Zeph. 2:2–3)

The prophet closes with hope for a faithful remnant whom God will restore (Zeph. 3:9–20). Only the humble will dwell with God. Thereby, God calls us to repentance and self-examination, exhorting us not to trust in human structures but in submission to his kingdom structures.

To recap, Zephaniah characterizes the day of the Lord as follows:

- Fiery wrath
- Devastation and darkness
- Bloodshed of living creatures and humanity
- Submission to God's sovereign judgment
- Impotence of material wealth

Amos on the Day of the Lord's Wrath

Amos prophesied during the mid-eighth century B.C., mostly against the northern kingdom of Israel, which became self-deceived in indulgence and idolatry (Amos 2:6–9:10). He delivered jolt-preaching oracles of categorical divine righteousness. Regrettably, his audience loved their sin more than their covenant-loving God. The northern kingdom of Israel was experiencing peace and prosperity, which provided a matrix for neglecting God's law and serving other idols. They deceived themselves by thinking they could be blessed by God with their external religious ritualism while disregarding his righteous demands. But God would have none of that.

> I absolutely despise your festivals! I get no pleasure from your religious assemblies! Even if you offer me burnt and grain offerings, I will not be satisfied; I will not look with favor on your peace offerings of fattened calves. (Amos 5:21–22)

Amos further denounced Israel for oppressing the poor and practicing bribery. Israel's delusions led to the brazen assumption that the day of the Lord would be a time of anticipated blessings for them. He challenged them in unqualified terms that it will be a period of judgment, not jubilation for the unrepentant.

> Woe to those who wish for the day of the Lord! Why do you want the Lord's day of judgment to come? It will bring darkness, not light. Disaster will be inescapable, as if a man ran from a lion only to meet a bear, then escaped into a house, leaned his hand against the wall, and was bitten by a poisonous snake. Don't you realize the Lord's day of judgment will bring darkness, not light—gloomy blackness, not bright light? (Amos 5:18–20)

Amos' prophecy was fulfilled in 722 B.C. when the northern kingdom fell, but it serves as a type for the eschatological day of the Lord. Amos' message is a palpable lesson transcending to our generation. The northern kingdom had developed a popular eschatology that assumed that, since they were the chosen ones, the great day of the Lord would be for "those godless nations."

But Amos assures them that God's enemies are not just nations that oppose Israel, but nations that oppose God himself. This included rebellious Israel. The northern kingdom had fostered the notion that they could have a privileged status while relying on their laurels from being God's covenant people. They presumed upon God's holiness, thinking they could placate God in their religious ritualism.

Accordingly, it would be a mistake for us to quickly judge their delusional foolishness. We are compelled to ask ourselves if we have worldly attachments that lull us into similar self-deception. Are we confusing some past or present religious externality such as the sinner's prayer, baptism, confirmation, tithing, or some other deed with a genuine union with Christ? We should seek God in sustained prayer to reveal our souls before him. The Lord draws near to those who seek him with a pure heart. Testing—not assuming—our salvation is a biblical command:

Jesus: "Not everyone who says to me, 'Lord, Lord,' will enter into the kingdom of heaven—only the one who does the will of my Father in heaven." (Matt. 7:21; cf. vv. 24–27)

Paul: Do you not know that the unrighteous will not inherit the kingdom of God? Do not be deceived! (1 Cor. 6:9)

James: What good is it, my brothers and sisters, if someone claims to have faith but does not have works? Can this kind of faith save him? (James 2:14)

Peter: Make every effort to be sure of your calling and election. (2 Pet. 1:10)

John: The person who keeps his commandments resides in God, and God in him. Now by this we know that God resides in us: by the Spirit he has given us. (1 John 3:24)

To recap, Amos warns:

- Be possessors of faith, not mere professors
- Moral ignorance not an excuse on judgment day

Joel, Isaiah, Obadiah, Zephaniah, and Amos are five prophets who display a foreboding picture of God's eschatological wrath. However, they are not the last word on what the day of the Lord entails. The progressive revelation given in the New Testament will complete our picture.

Jesus on Back-to-Back Rapture and Wrath

There is a pattern in Scripture of God supernaturally rescuing his people just before he executes divine judgment on the wicked. This is memorably attested in the story of God's plagues against Egypt, culminating in the deliverance of Israel from the hands of Pharaoh's army that was ultimately destroyed in the Red Sea. This pattern is continued in the context of the eschatological day of the Lord when Paul gives believers the reassuring promise: "For God did not destine us for wrath but for gaining salvation through our Lord Jesus Christ" (1 Thess. 5:9). The term for "salvation" in this verse is *sōtēria*. It has two common meanings: salvation in the sense of physical deliverance and salvation in the sense of non-physical deliverance (such as spiritual salvation). Here it takes on the former meaning since this promise is in the context of the rapture and the day of the Lord; thus, for believers, the day of the Lord will not "overtake you like a thief" (1 Thess. 5:4).

This pattern of deliverance before God's eschatological wrath is especially seen in Jesus' teaching where he emphasizes the back-to-back nature of deliverance and judgment.

> "The days are coming when you will desire to see one of the days of the Son of Man, and you will not see it. Then people will say to you, 'Look, there he is!' or 'Look, here he is!' Do not go out or chase after them. For just like the lightning flashes and lights up the sky from one side to the other, so will the Son of Man be in his day. But first he must suffer many things and be rejected by this generation. Just as it was in the days of Noah, so too it will be in the days of the Son of Man.

> People were eating, they were drinking, they were marrying, they were being given in marriage—*right up to the day Noah entered the ark*. Then the flood came and destroyed them all." (Luke 17:22–27, emphasis mine; cf. Matt. 24:37–41)

In this passage, there are at least three important truths regarding Christ's return. First, the sign of his second coming will be like lightning that will light up the sky. In Part 2, we covered this in our examination of the Olivet Discourse (Matt. 24:3, 27, 30). This will be his Shekinah glory announcing his divine presence to the entire world. Second, Jesus likens unbelievers at the time of the flood to unbelievers at the time of his second coming. Jesus says people were going on with their everyday affairs of eating, drinking, marrying, and being given in marriage. He does not make reference to gluttony, drunkenness, and immorality. To be sure, the antediluvian world was egregiously God-hating and self-loving (Gen. 6:11–13), and it is safe to assume that they were engaging in gluttony, drunkenness, and immorality (2 Pet. 2:5). But that is not the point Jesus makes here. He is highlighting that they were going on with their everyday activities, indifferent and oblivious of God's coming wrath. In short, the people of Noah's day were unprepared when the flood came. So will it be in the days at the coming of Christ. People will be going on with their everyday business, living only to please themselves. Paul is consistent with this truth, teaching that at the onset of the day of the Lord unbelievers will be saying, "'peace and security,' then sudden destruction comes on them, like labor pains on a pregnant woman, and they will surely not escape" (1 Thess. 5:3). The third point Jesus makes is that this obliviousness occurred "right up to the day" Noah entered the ark. The same day they entered, the flood began, not two days or five days or seven days later. The deluge began the very day Noah and his family entered the ark and shut the door (see Genesis 7:1–18). Noah was told that he had seven days to corral all the animals because "in seven days I will cause it to rain" (Gen. 7:4). At the end of the seven days, "all the fountains of the great deep burst open and the floodgates of the heavens were opened" (Gen. 7:11). This happened "on that very day Noah entered the ark" (Gen. 7:13). There will be no gap of days, weeks, or months, between the deliverance of the righteous and the unleashing of God's wrath at his return. It will be back to back.

To make sure he is not misunderstood about this truth, Jesus emphasizes this point by citing the episode of Lot and Sodom.

> "Likewise, just as it was in the days of Lot, people were eating, drinking, buying, selling, planting, building; but *on the day* Lot went out from Sodom, fire and sulfur rained down from heaven and destroyed them all. *It will be the same on the day* the Son of Man is revealed. *On that day*, anyone who is on the roof, with his goods in the house, must not come down to take them away, and likewise the person in the field must not turn back. Remember Lot's wife! Whoever tries to keep his life will lose it, but whoever loses his life will preserve it. I tell you, in that night there will be two people in one bed; one will be taken and the other left. There will be two women grinding grain together; one will be taken and the other left." (Luke 17:28–35, emphasis mine)

In the days of Lot—just as in the days of Noah—people were going on with their everyday tasks, "eating, drinking, buying, selling, planting, building." They were unaware and unprepared for God's impending judgment. His judgment began on the same day of Lot's deliverance. "On the day Lot went out from Sodom, fire and sulfur rained down from heaven and destroyed them all" (cf. Gen. 19:23–28). Accordingly, it "will be the same on the day the Son of Man is revealed."

Paul makes this similar point in 2 Thessalonians 1:7: "and to you who are being afflicted to give rest together with us when the Lord Jesus is revealed from heaven with his mighty angels." He instructs that the church will experience affliction right up to the initial day of the revelation of Christ. We know from his previous teaching in his first Thessalonian epistle that this deliverance is the rapture (1 Thess. 4:15–18). In 2 Thessalonians 1:10, he teaches that the exclusion of unbelievers from the presence of the Lord will begin "when he comes to be glorified among his saints and admired on that day among all who have believed." So for believers alive at that time "who believe our testimony" (v. 10), that day will begin eternal rest; but for unbelievers who "do not obey the gospel" (v. 8), it will begin eternal unrest. In other words, there will not be any delay between the rapture of the righteous and the day of the Lord's judgment upon the ungodly. The Lord's coming will be simultaneously twofold.

This "same day" truth contains significant implications because when Scripture teaches that there will be events happening before the day of the Lord, then by necessity these events—the celestial event (Joel 2:30–31), Elijah's coming (Mal. 4:5), and the apostasy and the revelation of the Antichrist (2 Thess. 2:1–4)—will happen before the rapture.

Rapture and the Day of the Lord Back-to-Back Events

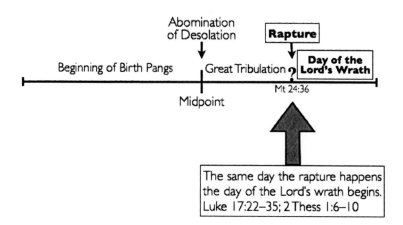

Paul on the Day of the Lord's Wrath

In his first epistle to the Thessalonians, the apostle Paul furnished us with one of the most important biblical teachings on the day of the Lord's wrath.

> Now on the topic of times and seasons, brothers and sisters, you have no need for anything to be written to you. For you know quite well that the day of the Lord will come in the same way as a thief in the night. Now when they are saying, "There is peace and security," then sudden destruction comes on them, like labor pains on a pregnant woman, and they will surely not escape. But you, brothers and sisters, are not in the darkness for the day to overtake you like a thief would. For you all are sons of the light and sons of the day. We are not of the night nor of the darkness. So then we must not sleep as the rest, but must stay alert and sober. For those who sleep, sleep at night and those who get drunk are drunk at night. But since we are of the day, we must stay sober by putting on the breastplate of faith and love and as a helmet our hope for salvation. For God did not destine us for wrath but for gaining salvation through our Lord Jesus Christ. He died for us so that whether we are alert or asleep we will come to life together with him. Therefore encourage one another and build up each other, just as you are in fact doing. (1 Thess. 5:1–11)

In 1 Thessalonians 4:13–18, Paul responded to the hopeless grieving of the Thessalonians by correcting an important point in their eschatology. But that is not the only element in their eschatology causing them to think wrongly. The Thessalonians were feeling trepidation that they might experience divine judgment; accordingly, in 1 Thessalonians 5:1–11, Paul reassures them of God's promise and sovereignty.

Paul introduces 1 Thessalonians 5:1–11 with the Greek phrase *peri de* ("now on the topic"). This phrase suggests that a question was raised by the Thessalonians, indicating further confusion in their defective eschatology. *Peri de* does not mean that Paul is now introducing a topic that is unrelated to his previous discussion on the parousia. Its technical meaning is not "what comes before it is disconnected from what comes after it." This phrase simply means Paul is beginning to shift to another perspective or topic that can be related to what came before. Only context can inform us as to the nature of the shift, not the phrase itself. In this context, we shall see that Paul is not addressing two completely different topics; instead, he continues his discussion of the return of the Lord, showing its effects upon the godly and the ungodly. In the previous passage on the rapture, Paul comforts the Thessalonian believers about the destiny of their dead loved ones. Now he turns to exhort these same believers about their *own* position in Christ in light of his parousia, teaching them to have spiritual watchfulness. With reference to unbelievers, he explains, they will not be able to escape the sudden return of the Lord—they will experience his eschatological wrath. Another reason we know Paul is continuing his instruction on the parousia in 1 Thessalonians 5:1–11 is given by Douglas J. Moo:

> [O]bserve how Paul speaks of "times and dates" in verse 1 without specifying the time or date of *what*. The omission of any specific event here could indicate that the previous topic is in mind. (emphasis his)[41]

So we should keep in mind that chapter breaks can be misleading, lest we think Paul is starting some completely new topic in chapter 5.[42]

Thief-Like Suddenness

> Now on the topic of times and seasons, brothers and sisters, you have no need for anything to be written to you. For you know quite well that the day of the Lord will come in the same way as a thief in the night. (1 Thess. 5:1–2)

By the time of the New Testament era, the two terms for "times" and "seasons" (*chronos* and *kairos*) became synonymous, so we should not read into this any temporal distinctions between the two. This is a literary feature called hendiadys, which is the use of two words to express a single idea for emphasis. We have similar expressions in our contemporary English—for example, "nice and easy" (cf. Dan 2:21; Acts 1:7).

Paul's statement "you have no need for anything to be written to you" indicates two things: (1) a question had arisen about the times and seasons of Christ's return, and (2) the Thessalonians had been previously instructed on this matter (e.g. 2 Thess. 2:5). On a surface level, it may be thought that Paul is rebuffing their question about the timing of the Lord's coming, as if they were asking, "Paul, what day is Jesus coming back?" with Paul replying, "I cannot tell you since he is coming back as a thief." This is a careless reading of the context. The Thessalonians are not asking for some specific calendric year-day-hour timing; rather, Paul's answer reveals that they are asking about a *conditional* when. In other words, Paul is teaching that Jesus will come back when a particular condition exists in the world. I will return to this point in a moment.

Paul explains why he does not need to write them about the times and seasons: "for you know quite well that the day of the Lord will come in the same way as a thief in the night." Evidently, Paul used this thief simile at the time he planted the Thessalonian church, but they did not grasp the full implications. The thief simile is frequently used in the New Testament, coined by Christ in his Olivet Discourse (see Matthew 24:43; Luke 12:39–40; cf. 2 Peter 3:10; Revelation 3:3; 16:15). How should we properly understand the intent of this simile? Pretribulationism erroneously imports into this thief imagery the theological system of imminence. But this imagery is not concerned with whether or not prophesied events must happen before Christ's return. Likewise, it is mistaken to read into the thief image the notion of unpredictability since Paul states, "But you, brothers and sisters, are not in the darkness for the day to overtake you like a thief would"

(1 Thess. 5:4). Instead, the image conveys a warning for *spiritual readiness*. Paul's point is that if you are not spiritually ready for Christ's return it will come upon you suddenly, with negative consequences. Obedience eliminates the possibility that our Lord will return as a thief to those who are watchful. We belong to Christ; hence we are to live with an attitude of expectancy—spiritual watchfulness. Paul develops this theme, drawing from his thief imagery.

> Now when they are saying, "There is peace and security," then sudden destruction comes on them, like labor pains on a pregnant woman, and they will surely not escape. But you, brothers and sisters, are not in the darkness for the day to overtake you like a thief would. (1 Thess. 5:3–4)

In verse 3, Paul teaches that sudden destruction for the ungodly is the result of the thief-like return of the Lord. He summarizes the perception of unbelievers when they say "peace and security." During the Antichrist's great tribulation, the world will experience peace and security for those who are loyal to him. Accordingly, Paul prophesies a conditional peace and security that will precede the day of the Lord. This peace and safety, however, will be illusory, a false security for unbelievers, because eventually unforeseen calamity will come upon them just as unexpected labor pains come upon a pregnant woman (cf. Matt. 24:37–39). Paul's analogy of labor pains is drawn from a day-of-the-Lord passage in Isaiah.

> Wail, for the Lord's day of judgment is near; it comes with all the destructive power of the sovereign judge. For this reason all hands hang limp, every human heart loses its courage. They panic—cramps and pain seize hold of them like those of a woman who is straining to give birth. They look at one another in astonishment; their faces are flushed red. Look, the Lord's day of judgment is coming; it is a day of cruelty and savage, raging anger, destroying the earth and annihilating its

sinners. Indeed the stars in the sky and their constellations no longer give out their light; the sun is darkened as soon as it rises, and the moon does not shine. (Isa. 13:6–10; see also Isaiah 26:17–21)

We should be careful not to confuse Paul's use of the birth pangs analogy with Jesus' purpose in using the same phrasing in the Olivet Discourse ("All these things are the beginning of birth pains," Matt. 24:8). Paul uses the phrase in a completely different application. Jesus applies the birth pangs metaphor to particular events *before* the Antichrist's great tribulation, while Paul applies it to the situation of the onset of the day of the Lord's wrath *after* the great tribulation.[43]

Next, since destruction will come suddenly like labor pangs, Paul says the ungodly "will surely not escape." Here we see a parallel with Luke, who also uses this "escape" language in the same context as the Lord's return.

"But be on your guard so that your hearts are not weighed down with dissipation and drunkenness [cf. 1 Thess. 5:6–8] and the worries of this life, and that day close down upon you suddenly like a trap. For it will overtake all who live on the face of the whole earth [cf. 1 Thess. 5:2–4]. But stay alert at all times [cf. 1 Thess. 5:6], praying that you may have strength to escape all these things that must happen [cf. 1 Thess. 5:3, 8], and to stand before the Son of Man." (Luke 21:34–36)

Furthering the parallel, Luke's "escape" language is found in the context of the celestial disturbances, as well (21:25–28). This parallel is strengthened when we consider that both the celestial disturbances and this same "escape" language are found during the sixth seal as the ungodly seek to escape the inescapable (Rev. 6:12–17).

One further mention should be Isaiah 26:17–21, which references both "birth pangs" and uses "escape" language, followed by a depiction of the resurrection of God's people escaping from his wrath:

As when a pregnant woman gets ready to deliver and strains and cries out because of her labor pains, so were we because of you, O Lord. We were pregnant, we strained, we gave birth, as it were, to wind. We cannot produce deliverance on the earth; people to populate the world are not born. Your dead will come back to life; your corpses will rise up. Wake up and shout joyfully, you who live in the ground! For you will grow like plants drenched with the morning dew, and the earth will bring forth its dead spirits. Go, my people! Enter your inner rooms! Close your doors behind you! Hide for a little while, until his angry judgment is over! For look, the LORD is coming out of the place where he lives, to punish the sin of those who live on the earth. The earth will display the blood shed on it; it will no longer cover up its slain. (cf. Isa. 13:6–10; Joel 2:30–32; Amos 9:1ff)

Stages of Birth Pangs

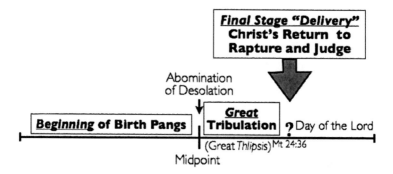

Returning to Paul's passage in verse 4, his reassurance to the Thessalonians implies that they were anxious that they might not escape the day of the Lord. To reassure them, Paul contrasts the ungodly, who will not escape because Christ is coming back as a thief for them, with the obedient-vigilant, who "are not in the darkness for the day to overtake you like a thief would." (This reassuring promise undermines the pretribulational notion that Jesus is secretly coming back as a thief for his church.) The meta-

phor of darkness refers to being apart from Christ and opposed
to God. Conversely, not being in darkness refers to the morality
of a child of God; thus by their nature, believers should be spiritually vigilant and prepared.

Be Watchful!

> For you all are sons of the light and sons of the day. We are not
> of the night nor of the darkness. So then we must not sleep as
> the rest, but must stay alert and sober. For those who sleep,
> sleep at night and those who get drunk are drunk at night.
> But since we are of the day, we must stay sober by putting on
> the breastplate of faith and love and as a helmet our hope for
> salvation. (1 Thess. 5:5–8)

Paul explains why Jesus is not coming back as a thief in the night
for believers. He elaborates on the contrast between two moral
natures. Verse 5 gives the reason: They are sons of light and day.
This metaphor of light-day refers to being part of the people of
God. The reference alludes to Jesus' words, "While you have the
light, believe in the light, so that you may become sons of light"
(John 12:36). But belonging to God is not merely static because
Paul will explain the moral implications of possessing this relationship with God. A child of God cannot belong to both the day
and the night, light and darkness, so he again emphasizes that
they are "not of the night nor of the darkness."

In verse 6, Paul gives the Thessalonians the moral inference
for belonging to God. First, they must not sleep. The term "sleep"
in this context is metaphorical, characterizing the lack of spiritual life of the unregenerate, just as "the rest" refers to their pagan
neighbors (cf. 1 Thess. 4:13). Thus, he exhorts believers to live in
the light of their God-given nature by staying spiritually "alert
and sober" and avoiding ethical lethargy. This vigilant and self-
controlled posture will be imperative as the Lord's coming nears
because it serves a vital purpose. During the Antichrist's great
tribulation, this readiness will be vital to overcoming the tempta-

tions of persecution, false teachings, and slothfulness, so that the believer may embrace the Lord at his coming blamelessly instead of in shame.

In contrast to the light-day nature of believers, Paul gives an additional description to the nature of unbelievers. "[T]hose who sleep, sleep at night and those who get drunk are drunk at night" (1 Thess. 5:7; cf. Luke 21:34). Paul may be using the term "drunk" as a synecdoche, which is a figure of speech in which a part is used to refer to the whole or vice versa. Paul literally refers to the sin of being drunk, but he likely is also referring to the whole complex of vices associated with drunkenness in the mind of the ancient person—laziness, adultery, coarse joking, greed, and so on. In antiquity, these were principally "night sins." Certainly today we can add to this list the idolatry of entertainment and sports in our culture, as well as addiction to the Internet and any other diversions that keep the Christian soul busy and distracted from kingdom work.

In verse 8, the apostle emphatically contrasts unbelievers with believers, reminding them again that they are of the day and thus to maintain soberness. How is this to be accomplished? He exhorts them to practice the three-corded rope that he couches in the military imagery of "putting on the breastplate of faith and love and as a helmet our hope for salvation." The implication is that if we stumble in these three Christian virtues, there is the danger of losing our soberness. The "hope of salvation" in this context in light of verse 9 likely refers not to our salvation in the common sense, but to deliverance from the coming day of the Lord's wrath, which, indeed, presupposes spiritual salvation (cf. 1 Thess. 1:3). Therefore, the closer we approach the Lord's coming, the more the devil will throw in our daily path distractions and sins to deflect our attention from our parousia-alertness. Let us consider well the apostle's warning. We can approach that day in confidence if we cling to biblical faith, love, and hope.

God's Gracious Decree of Deliverance

> For God did not destine us for wrath but for gaining salvation
> through our Lord Jesus Christ. He died for us so that whether
> we are alert or asleep we will come to life together with him.
> Therefore encourage one another and build up each other, just
> as you are in fact doing. (1 Thess. 5:9–11)

Paul shifts from the difference between the character of believers
and unbelievers to the destiny of believers. The sanctifying exhortations in verse 8 are grounded in the truth of verse 9, teaching that God does not destine Christians for wrath. Throughout
Paul's two Thessalonian letters, he stresses the sovereignty of God
in salvation. God's purposes are foremost, expressed through his
loving act of not destining his redeemed people unto wrath—
tribulation and trials, yes, but not divine wrath. The reason Paul
says we can have confidence in our salvation is because God has
"not destined us to wrath." In this context, Paul is not speaking
of eternal wrath, but the eschatological wrath that will be poured
upon the ungodly at Christ's return.

Finally, we are told that the purpose for Christ's death is so
we would be "together with him." God seeks to dwell with his
people. Reiterating the comforting truth of the believer's state,
Paul writes, "whether we are alert or asleep we will come to life
together with him" (cf. 1 Thess. 4:13–18). In that verse, it may
be better to render "alert" (*grēgoreō*) as "awake" in the physical
sense, harking back to Paul's earlier statement about those who
are found alive (i.e. "awake") at Jesus' parousia. Finally, in verse
11 there is a restatement of the same exhortation from the previous section: "Therefore encourage one another" (cf. 1 Thess.
4:18).

In summary, the Thessalonians asked about the times and
seasons of the day of the Lord. Paul explained that the timing
is based on a spiritual condition related through the simile of a
thief in the night. The day of the Lord will happen at a particular eschatological point when the ungodly are confidently saying

"peace and security," for then there will be sudden destruction. But watchful believers will be ready. Accordingly, 1 Thessalonians 5:1–11 is not teaching that we need to be ready and watchful because the day of the Lord is imminent; rather, Paul is reassuring them that they will not experience the day of the Lord's wrath. They need to be watchful and ready because the reassurance is *grounded* in their ordained redemptive status as God's people (1 Thess. 5:4–5, 8–10).[44]

Next, we will shift to our final section of the Bible addressing the day of the Lord's wrath, the book of Revelation. It will introduce us to the systematic elements of judgment that God will execute upon the world.

The Seventh Seal Pronounces Wrath

Jesus is the only one "worthy" (in other words, authorized) to break the seals in order to open the scroll and reclaim his earthly reign through conquering the nations that constitute the kingdom of darkness. The breaking of the seventh and final seal pronounces the day of the Lord's wrath. The opening of the scroll introduces the first phase of God's wrath in a series of trumpet judgments. This will be followed by the second phase, the finale of God's wrath through the seven bowl judgments and Armageddon.[45]

> Now when the Lamb opened the seventh seal there was silence in heaven for about half an hour. Then I saw the seven angels who stand before God, and seven trumpets were given to them. Another angel holding a golden censer came and was stationed at the altar. A large amount of incense was given to him to offer up, with the prayers of all the saints, on the golden altar that is before the throne. The smoke coming from the incense, along with the prayers of the saints, ascended before God from the angel's hand. Then the angel took the censer, filled it with fire from the altar, and threw it on the earth, and there were crashes of thunder, roaring, flashes of lightning,

and an earthquake. Now the seven angels holding the seven
trumpets prepared to blow them. (Rev. 8:1–6)

Before the first trumpet judgment is sounded, there is a
solemn scene in heaven as the seventh seal is opened—a silent
overture to the day of the Lord. This is the only place in the
book of Revelation that silence is mentioned. From a prewrath
perspective, this makes sense. The resurrection and rapture of
God's people just occurred (Rev. 7:9–17); now the day of the
Lord's wrath is about to be executed. This cosmic moment of
silence signals the fearsome wrath of God coming upon the
world. The prophet Zephaniah echoes this silence. "Be silent
before the Lord God, for the Lord's day of judgment is almost
here. The Lord has prepared a sacrificial meal; he has ritually
purified his guests" (Zeph. 1:7). And Zechariah writes, "Be
silent in the Lord's presence, all people everywhere, for he is
being moved to action in his holy dwelling place" (Zech. 2:13;
cf. Hab. 2:20). This silence serves God's judicial righteousness.
His judgments are true, holy, and blameless—no creature can
answer them![46]

Seven Tormenting Trumpets of God's Wrath

In the Old Testament, trumpets symbolized God's intervention
in the lives of his people. In our case, seven angels who stand
before God are each given a trumpet. The angels who "stand before God" are a special order of angels. In this context, trumpets
symbolize a judgment battle cry. (Incidentally, seven priests blew
seven trumpets in the fall of Jericho in Joshua 6:4–9.) We are told
that another angel came to the altar with a golden censer. The
angel was given much incense "to offer up, with the prayers of
all the saints, on the golden altar that is before the throne" (v. 3).
The incense offered along with prayers suggests that its purpose
was to please God so he would respond. Given this preparatory
context for judgment, these soon-to-be-answered prayers most
likely include the prayers of the fifth seal martyrs: "How long,

Sovereign Master, holy and true, before you judge those who live on the earth and avenge our blood?" (Rev. 6:9–10).

After the prayers reach God, the silence is broken as "the angel took the censer, filled it with fire from the altar, and threw it on the earth, and there were crashes of thunder, roaring, flashes of lightning, and an earthquake" (Rev. 8:5). These are standard elements of judgment theophany introducing the ensuing trumpet judgments. The censer previously served to offer up incense with the prayers of the saints; now it functions to avenge them. The forceful imagery of throwing fire upon the earth will be repeated in the trumpet judgments (Rev. 8:7–8). A great earthquake occurred at the sixth seal, and here we see another earthquake, with more to come. These earthquakes will remind the ungodly of God's sovereignty over the earth— or shall I say "under the earth"? We will later see this similar theophanic cluster in further instances (Rev. 11:19; 16:18; also 4:5). In short, the hurling of fire, thunder, roaring, lightning, and earthquake is God's cachet that it is now *his time*. There is no more delay, no more silence. The angels prepare to execute the judgments of God.

> The first angel blew his trumpet, and there was hail and fire mixed with blood, and it was thrown at the earth so that a third of the earth was burned up, a third of the trees were burned up, and all the green grass was burned up. (Rev. 8:7)

The first angel sounds his trumpet with judgment thrown down to earth as hail, fire, and blood devastate one-third of the vegetation. Similarly, God judged Egypt with hail and fire (Exod. 9:13–35). Here they are "mixed with blood," a judgment that scorches "a third" of the earth. A third is a distinguishing mark for the trumpet judgments.

There is a caveat in examining these judgments. It may be easy to implicitly view them as unrealistic events beyond our experiences and thereby interpret them as merely symbolic. We must resist this way of looking upon these depictions, for they are divinely decreed and thus will happen. Peter teaches the certainty of God's judgments calling us to repentance.

> Through these things the world existing at that time was destroyed when it was deluged with water. But by the same word the present heavens and earth have been reserved for fire, by being kept for the day of judgment and destruction of the ungodly. Now, dear friends, do not let this one thing escape your notice, that a single day is like a thousand years with the Lord and a thousand years are like a single day. The Lord is not slow concerning his promise, as some regard slowness, but is being patient toward you, because he does not wish for any to perish but for all to come to repentance. But the day of the Lord will come like a thief; when it comes, the heavens will disappear with a horrific noise, and the celestial bodies will melt away in a blaze, and the earth and every deed done on it will be laid bare. Since all these things are to melt away in this manner, what sort of people must we be, conducting our lives in holiness and godliness. (2 Pet. 3:6–11)

Next, the second trumpet portrays a great mountain of fire:

> Then the second angel blew his trumpet, and something like a great mountain of burning fire was thrown into the sea. A third of the sea became blood, and a third of the creatures living in the sea died, and a third of the ships were completely destroyed. (Rev. 8:8–9)

There are two possible scenarios in this judgment. First, it may be that the great mountain burning of fire describes a volcano. It could be a super volcano, since it says it will kill one-third of sea life and any ships upon the waters. Super volcanoes are found both on land and on the bottom of the ocean. Second, this could be a large meteor. The text says "something *like* [*hōs*] a great mountain of burning fire." The simile would point to something that resembles a great mountain of burning fire that was "thrown into the sea." This may refer to a trajectory of a meteor. Either a super volcano or meteor are plausible scenarios.

Next, the third trumpet describes a huge burning star:

> Then the third angel blew his trumpet, and a huge star burning like a torch fell from the sky; it landed on a third of the rivers and on the springs of water. (Now the name of the star is Wormwood.) So a third of the waters became wormwood [bitter], and many people died from these waters because they were poisoned. (Rev. 8:10–11)

The scope of this judgment is upon one-third of inland waters. Here we have a graphic description of a meteor ("star") blazing in the sky, eventually crashing to the ground and poisoning the inland waters. The highest likelihood is that this is a meteor. If so, this implies that the second trumpet judgment is more likely a volcano than a meteor.

The star has the name "Wormwood" (*Apsinthos*), a bitter-tasting herb with medicinal value for killing intestinal worms. The effect of the meteor is that it will cause one-third of the inland waters to be undrinkable. Going without food is one thing, but the lack of water results in a quick, inevitable death. Presumably, inhabitants in this one-third of the land will not immediately drink from it. The situation will get desperate, and "many people" will die attempting to hydrate their bodies. Such a judgment is unfathomable for moderns who take municipal conveniences for granted. There is a pragmatic warning in this judgment prophecy—repent and worship the Creator who sustains all life.

Next, the fourth trumpet affects the heavenly bodies:

> Then the fourth angel blew his trumpet, and a third of the sun was struck, and a third of the moon, and a third of the stars, so that a third of them were darkened. And there was no light

for a third of the day and for a third of the night likewise. (Rev. 8:12)

The scope of this trumpet judgment is the darkening of one-third of the celestial luminaries, keeping with the one-third pattern of the previous three trumpet judgments. The language suggests this will not be an eclipse, but something more ominous. It will not be a gradual darkening since the Greek term used for "struck" is *plēssō*, meaning "to strike with force." Neither will this be a partial darkness as "a third of the sun" may suggest, because the second half of the verse clarifies that it will be complete darkness *during* the extended one-third duration. When this happens, no one will be able to tell the difference between day and night; they will be indistinguishable. The previous trumpet judgments executed fire, hail, destruction, and death. The fourth trumpet judgment will engender confusion and abject fear due to the disruption from the lack of any natural light (cf. Rev. 16:10).

Will this one-third darkening occur only a single time or for several days, weeks, or months? We cannot be sure since the text does not say. The darkening of the celestial bodies is a frequent characteristic of God's eschatological judgment. Most recently, we saw it in the darkness at the sixth seal, functioning to announce the impending day of the Lord's wrath. In this trumpet judgment, darkness serves as the principle element in God's judgment.

Three 'Woe' Trumpets

Then I looked, and I heard an eagle flying directly overhead, proclaiming with a loud voice, "Woe! Woe! Woe to those who live on the earth because of the remaining sounds of the trumpets of the three angels who are about to blow them!" (Rev. 8:13)

Each of the first four trumpet judgments is centered on some aspect of nature—vegetation, the ocean, inland waters, and celestial bodies, respectively. The last three trumpet judgments intensify in punishment specifically against the inhabitants of the earth; hence the threefold woes. John sees an eagle flying in the sky proclaiming warnings of sorrow and distress upon those who live on the earth. The term for "directly overhead" is *mesouranēma*, which means "a point or region of the sky directly above the earth—high in the sky, midpoint in the sky, directly overhead, straight above in the sky."[47] This is reflected in three aspects: (1) supernatural: through a messenger eagle; (2) visible: a point in the sky that cannot be missed; and (3) audible: with a "loud voice." The first four trumpets are unmistakably divine wrath. But the remaining three trumpet judgments progressively heighten the punishment.

Fifth Trumpet (First Woe)

> Then the fifth angel blew his trumpet, and I saw a star that had fallen from the sky to the earth, and he was given the key to the shaft of the abyss. He opened the shaft of the abyss and smoke rose out of it like smoke from a giant furnace. The sun and the air were darkened with smoke from the shaft. Then out of the smoke came locusts onto the earth, and they were given power like that of the scorpions of the earth. They were told not to damage the grass of the earth, or any green plant or tree, but only those people who did not have the seal of God on their forehead. The locusts were not given permission to kill them, but only to torture them for five months, and their torture was like that of a scorpion when it stings a person. In those days people will seek death, but will not be able to find it; they will long to die, but death will flee from them. Now the locusts looked like horses equipped for battle. On their heads were something like crowns similar to gold, and their faces looked like men's faces. They had hair like women's hair, and their teeth were like lions' teeth. They had breastplates like iron breastplates, and the sound of their wings was like the noise of many horse-drawn chariots charging into battle. They

> have tails and stingers like scorpions, and their ability to injure people for five months is in their tails. They have as king over them the angel of the abyss, whose name in Hebrew is *Abaddon*, and in Greek, *Apollyon*. (Rev. 9:1–11)

The biblical description of the fifth and sixth trumpets is lengthier than the first four trumpets, probably for highlighting the intensity and objects of wrath. The fifth trumpet judgment is the most freakish, portraying a demonic locust invasion torturing humankind for five months. The narrative opens with John seeing "a star that had fallen from the sky to the earth, and he was given the key to the shaft of the abyss." Stars can symbolize angels (e.g. Rev. 1:20). In addition, the text indicates that a figure is in view since it says, "[H]e was given the key." I assume this is a demonic angel since the biblical concept of angels falling from the sky refers to fallen demonic angels.[48] The "abyss" (i.e. netherworld) designates the deep place in the earth for the abode of the dead waiting for judgment (Ps. 63:9; Rom. 10:7). It also serves as a prison for selected evil spirits (Luke 8:31; Matt. 8:29; Rev. 9:2–11; 11:7; 17:8; 20:1–3; cf. 2 Pet. 2:4; Jude 6; 1 Enoch 10:4–6; 18:11–16). The key that opens and closes the shaft represents God's sovereign time and purposes in which he either permits evil beings to carry out their demonic activities or fetters them.

Next, the angel opens the shaft of the abyss, causing smoke to rise out of it. The dense smoke is described as if it were coming from a giant furnace, darkening the sun and air. The text states, "[O]ut of the smoke came locusts onto the earth." From this thick smoke comes frightening (demonic) creatures described as locusts. The expression "out of the smoke . . . onto the earth" reveals their supernatural character. They do not possess power of themselves, however, and must be "given power like that of the scorpions of the earth" (v. 3). The comparison to scorpions refers to their ability to cause excruciating stings. The irony is that these demonic beings who hate God will be doing his will by judging the ungodly!

Verse 4 tells us, "They [locust-demons] were told not to damage the grass of the earth, or any green plant or tree, but only those people who did not have the seal of God on their forehead." The passage does not state who gave them directives; however, the verb *errethē* ("they were told") is in the passive voice, which suggests God's sovereign directive. Further, these locust creatures have over them an abyss angel-king, who in return is also subjected to God's sovereign command (Rev. 9:11).

In the first trumpet judgment, the object of destruction was vegetation. "[A] third of the trees were burned up, and all the green grass was burned up." Now the fifth trumpet judgment presupposes that the vegetation grew back since there is a command not to damage it (v. 4). The locust-demons are commanded to hurt only those people who do not have the seal of God on their foreheads. Those who do have the seal of God are the 144,000 physical Jews, who are protected from God's wrath (see Revelation 7:1–3). In verse 5, the locusts are restricted from killing but have permission to torture the inhabitants of the earth like "a scorpion." This term for "torture" (*basanismos*) is one of the strongest words in the Bible for pain or suffering. There is also a restriction on how long they can torture—five months, which may suggest that this suffering will last unusually longer than the other judgments. Accordingly, the day of the Lord must begin at least five months before the end of the seven-year period. (Incidentally, this point is problematic for the version of posttribulationism that places the day of the Lord at the very end of the seven-year period.) To be stung a single time would be painful, but to be stung multiple times over a five-month period will be unbearable. It is no wonder this severe infliction of pain will cause the wicked to "seek death, but . . . not be able to find it; they will long to die, but death will flee from them" (Rev. 9:6). God will supernaturally prevent them from killing themselves to avoid their punishment for their idolatry and rejection of the Creator.

The torture the wicked will receive is bad enough, but apprehension of it will cause bitter anguish. John describes the hideous creatures involved in this judgment.

Now the locusts looked like horses equipped for battle. On
their heads were something like crowns similar to gold, and
their faces looked like men's faces. They had hair like women's
hair, and their teeth were like lions' teeth. They had breastplates like iron breastplates, and the sound of their wings was
like the noise of many horse-drawn chariots charging into battle. They have tails and stingers like scorpions, and their ability
to injure people for five months is in their tails. They have as
king over them the angel of the abyss, whose name in Hebrew
is *Abaddon*, and in Greek, *Apollyon*. (Rev. 9:7–11)

This passage contains the highest concentration of similes in the
book of Revelation (*hōs, homoias* "as," "like"). The head of the locust resembles a horse, and the locusts look like horses equipped
for battle aiming to inflict pain on their targets. The gold-like
"crowns" on their heads may symbolize conquering and/or authority, albeit an earthly authority that will eventually come to an
end with their own punishment. The faces of the locusts look like
men's faces (*prosōpa anthrōpōn*), which could also be rendered
"human faces." A common interpretation is that these grotesque
demon-creatures possess some human traits. If that is the case, it
is hard to tell what those traits will be.

The next set of these creaturely comparisons depicts "hair
like women's hair, and their teeth were like lions' teeth." Their
tails will inflict pain, but their evidently long hair and large teeth
reinforce the dread of being attacked (for a typological reference,
see Joel 1:6–7; 2:4–5). Next, they have breastplates like iron conveying invincibility, and the foreboding sound of their wings is
like that of a multitude of horse-drawn chariots going into battle.
Verse 10 restates verse 5: "They have tails and stingers like scorpions, and their ability to injure people for five months is in their
tails." Here we are told specifically that they will afflict people
through their tail-stingers.

Concluding the fifth trumpet judgment, the locust creatures
"have as king over them the angel of the abyss, whose name in
Hebrew is *Abaddon*, and in Greek, *Apollyon*" (Rev. 9:11). The

name means "destroyer." This angel-king's sole purpose is to destroy lives. There are various opinions as to his identity: (1) the same one who was given the key to the shaft of the abyss; (2) a fallen angel who lives within the abyss and rules over all of these demonic locusts; (3) Satan himself; and (4) a demonic archangel or "lieutenant" under Satan. Regardless of this angel's identity, the locust-creatures will be organized and ruled with a demonic strategy of torturing the wicked. It will not be arbitrary or chaotic. It will be planned and devious.

Sixth Trumpet (Second Woe)

> The first woe has passed, but two woes are still coming after these things! Then the sixth angel blew his trumpet, and I heard a single voice coming from the horns on the golden altar that is before God, saying to the sixth angel, the one holding the trumpet, "Set free the four angels who are bound at the great river Euphrates!" Then the four angels who had been prepared for this hour, day, month, and year were set free to kill a third of humanity. The number of soldiers on horseback was two hundred million; I heard their number. Now this is what the horses and their riders looked like in my vision: The riders had breastplates that were fiery red, dark blue, and sulfurous yellow in color. The heads of the horses looked like lions' heads, and fire, smoke, and sulfur came out of their mouths. A third of humanity was killed by these three plagues, that is, by the fire, the smoke, and the sulfur that came out of their mouths. For the power of the horses resides in their mouths and in their tails, because their tails are like snakes, having heads that inflict injuries. The rest of humanity, who had not been killed by these plagues, did not repent of the works of their hands, so that they did not stop worshiping demons and idols made of gold, silver, bronze, stone, and wood—idols that cannot see or hear or walk about. Furthermore, they did not repent of their murders, of their magic spells, of their sexual immorality, or of their stealing. (Rev. 9:12–21)

The fifth trumpet inaugurated the first woe, characterized by torture. The sixth trumpet represents the second woe, resulting in death to one-third of humankind. There will not be a respite for the ungodly. At the sixth trumpet, John heard a "single voice coming from the horns on the golden altar that is before God, saying to the sixth angel, the one holding the trumpet, 'Set free the four angels who are bound at the great river Euphrates!'" We are not told whose voice is coming from the horns, but the text indicates God's sovereign authority to execute the release of the four bound angels. The same angel who sounds the trumpet is also given authority to release the four angels. The passage is unclear whether these are good or evil angels, but "bound" does befit demonic angels (cf. Rev. 20:2). In addition, the four angels seem to be the "generals" of the two hundred million horsemen. These four have been bound "at the great river Euphrates." The river demarcated the eastern boundary of the ancient Roman Empire. The reference to the Euphrates connotes judgment, particularly on ancient Israel, since foreign armies crossed over it (cf. Rev. 16:12).

These four angels were "prepared" for this time to "kill a third of humanity." God is not arbitrary in the nature of his judgment and the timing of its execution. He is sovereign over all. The four ascending time designations (hour, day, month, and year) underscore God's control and his all-wise, predetermined timing. It is almost inconceivable that there will be a day when one-third of humanity will perish. Assuming our population today, the sixth trumpet judgment would extirpate two billion unrepentant humans. No wonder it is called the second woe! Lest we forget, God once wiped out all of humanity, except for Noah's family-remnant. There will be a second time in human history when the world's depravity will reach its full strength and God will say, "No more!" (2 Pet. 3:6–7).

Next, in Revelation 9:16 the number of soldiers on horseback are two hundred million. The passage does not say where these millions of soldiers come from. Evidently, they are associated with the four angels who are their leaders. John says, "I heard their number," which may be his way of confirming this incredible number. These troops are likely demonic, not human, because of their sheer number and association with supernatural horses.

If the immensity of the number of troops is not enough, the description of them and their horses in verses 17–19 will complete this grotesque picture. The reader will notice similarities between the demonic cavalry mentioned here and the demonic locusts mentioned back in verses 7–10. In the Greek, there is some debate about whether it is the horses or the riders who wear the breastplates of "fiery red, dark blue, and sulfurous yellow." It is more likely the riders, but it may refer to both. In any event, the colors are intended to induce terror, as are the heads of the horses looking like "lions' heads." Out of their mouths will be "fire, smoke, and sulfur," indicating their demonic nature. Fire, smoke, and sulfur are God's instruments for striking down one-third of humanity. The power of the horses is found in their mouths, and their tails are like "snakes having heads that inflict injuries."

During the great tribulation, authority from the fourth seal is given to kill over one-fourth of the earth (*gē*), suggesting that not all are killed; rather, authority is given over a *realm* (Rev. 6:8–9). In contrast, during the day of the Lord, this sixth trumpet judgment specifically kills one-third of humanity (*anthrōpos*), for they will not escape death—a certainty of being killed rather than the threat of being killed (Rev. 9:18).

The remaining two-thirds who are not killed refuse to repent of their murders, magic spells, sexual immorality, thievery, and worship of demons and idols. This demonstrates that without the grace of God, sinful humans are hardened in their sin. We can infer that the wicked during Noah's day were cursing God—not repenting—as they were drowning in the flood. Simply recognizing God's sovereignty is not sufficient for salvation; the heart must be regenerated by the Spirit to bring about repentance and saving faith. Cursing God will characterize the world's response to his just acts in his day. God will smash idolaters, resulting in praise for executing his justice upon them (Rev. 11:15–18). It would be a mistake to see these judgments as a divine "offer" for repentance. This is not their purpose. They are intended to *judge*. God has the freedom to bring down his judgment at any time upon the ungodly. He is not restricted to waiting until they die (e.g. 2 Thess. 2:10–12). In fact, the seven churches are called upon to repent before it is too late (Revelation 2–3). In addition, the apostle Peter compares the flood judgment to the future certainty of the day of the Lord's wrath, emphasizing the motivation for repentance and holy living at *this present time* (2 Pet. 3:5–12).

Six Trumpets:
First Phase of the Day of the Lord's Wrath

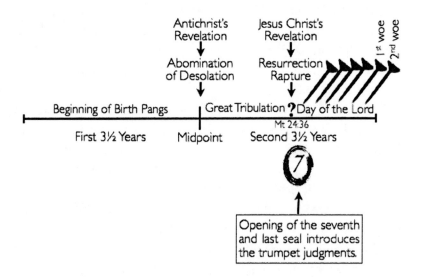

We now will consider the second phase—the culmination—of the day of the Lord's wrath, which is manifested in the bowl judgments and includes the battle of Armageddon. This last set of judgments will exterminate what is remaining of the beast's kingdom, reclaiming God's kingdom on earth for Christ's rule.

Seventh Trumpet (Third Woe)

The completion of the sixth trumpet takes us to the end of the seven-year period, which is then followed by thirty- and forty-five-day periods (cf. Dan. 12:9–13). Soon after the seven-year period is complete, the seventh trumpet will blow, announcing God's reclamation of his reign on earth. The seventh trumpet is the third woe, which marks the highest intensity of the day of the Lord's wrath manifested through the seven bowl judgments. But first is a pronouncement of God's reclamation of his reign on earth.

> The second woe has come and gone; the third is coming quickly. Then the seventh angel blew his trumpet, and there were loud voices in heaven saying: "The kingdom of the world has become the kingdom of our Lord and of his Christ, and he will reign for ever and ever." (Rev. 11:14–15; cf. Dan. 2:44)

The "kingdom of the world" is none other than Satan's kingdom manifested through his minion, the Antichrist. The Antichrist will be given 1,260 days of authority to rule the world and persecute God's people (Dan. 7:25; Rev. 13:5). This authority starts at the midpoint of the seven-year period, causing him to commit the abomination of desolation (Dan. 9:27). When his authority expires at the conclusion of the seven-year period, God will formally reclaim his earthly kingdom from Satan at the blowing of the seventh trumpet (Rev. 11:15). During the thirty-day period, the bowl judgments will function to execute the pronouncement of God's kingdom and the demise of the Antichrist's kingdom. The bowls are instrumental in the transitional phase, replacing the Antichrist's rule with Christ's rule.

This transition, however, will not go unopposed by the Antichrist. He will refuse to accept Jesus' authority as king at the seventh-trumpet pronouncement. The Antichrist is not going to raise the white flag and hand over his kingdom just like that. After his authority of 42 months expires, he will attempt (unsuccessfully) to keep his authority, kingdom, and followers by waging war against Christ. He is going to fight it out, even though his divinely given authority has expired. The first act of King Jesus, therefore, is to wipe out his enemies who oppose his kingdom through the bowl judgments and the battle of Armageddon, where the Antichrist's ultimate destruction is realized (Rev. 19:20).

Seven Blitzing Bowls and Battle of Armageddon

The trumpet judgments require a substantive time to unfold; for example, we saw that the fifth trumpet lasts five months. In contrast, the nature and purpose of the bowl judgments will unfold rapidly during the thirty days that follow the seven-year period. The prophet Daniel provides evidence of an additional thirty-day period following the seven-year period. The abomination of desolation will last thirty additional days after the completion of the Antichrist's authority of 1,260 days. "From the time that the daily sacrifice is removed and the abomination that causes desolation is set in place, there are 1,290 days [an additional thirty days]" (Dan. 12:11). At the completion of this thirty-day period, the end of the desolation will coincide with the destruction of the desolator (the Antichrist).

> And he [the Antichrist] will make a firm covenant with the many for one week [seven years], but in the middle of the week he will put a stop to sacrifice and grain offering; and on the wing of abominations will come one who makes desolate [the Antichrist], even *until a complete destruction, one that is decreed, is poured out on the one who makes desolate* [the Antichrist] (Dan. 9:27 NASB, emphasis mine).

This destruction of the desolator-Antichrist is depicted in the aftermath of Armageddon.

> Then I saw the beast and the kings of the earth and their armies assembled to do battle with the one who rode the horse

and with his army. Now the beast was seized, and along with him the false prophet who had performed the signs on his behalf—signs by which he deceived those who had received the mark of the beast and those who worshiped his image. Both of them were thrown alive into the lake of fire burning with sulfur. (Rev. 19:20)

Accordingly, the bowls, including the battle of Armageddon, will unfold during the brief thirty-day period.

The briefness of God's final wrath is also conveyed in the use of the imagery of the bowls. The New Testament mentions at least fifteen different jars, bowls, baskets, and other types of vessels. However, the term for this particular "bowl" is *phialē*, which means a "broad, shallow bowl."[49] This choice of imagery is not arbitrary but connotes swift judgment. It suggests that emptying the contents of God's final wrath will happen swiftly. This imagery evokes a salvo of bowl judgments emptied until they are completed, like a grand finale to a fireworks display. Thus, it fits well for the brief thirty-day period.

The first bowl states,

> Then I heard a loud voice from the temple declaring to the seven angels: "Go and pour out on the earth the seven bowls containing God's wrath." So the first angel went and poured out his bowl on the earth. Then ugly and painful sores appeared on the people who had the mark of the beast and who worshiped his image. (Rev. 16:1–2)

The loud commissioning of the seven angels to pour out the wrath of God is aimed at the beast-marked worshipers. Those who took the mark of the beast and thereby worshiped his image will suffer the plague of ugly, painful sores (cf. Exod. 9:9–11). The suffering from these sores under this first bowl will be excruciating. Imagine the torment of sores all over the body, not being able to sit or lie down, or even walk! Giving allegiance to the adversary of God will be the ultimate act of idolatry; hence the pervasive warnings in Revelation not to take the mark.

The second bowl states,

> Next, the second angel poured out his bowl on the sea and it turned into blood, like that of a corpse, and every living creature that was in the sea died. (Rev. 16:3)

The first bowl was directed toward the earth, while the second bowl targets the sea. In contrast to the trumpets, which affect only portions of the earth and sea, the bowls target the entirety of both. In this case, the sea is turned entirely into blood, causing every living creature within it to die (cf. Exod. 7:14–21). Every sea creature will perish! This enormous devastation will bring the world trade economy immediately to its knees.

The third bowl states,

> Then the third angel poured out his bowl on the rivers and the springs of water, and they turned into blood. Now I heard the angel of the waters saying: "You are just—the one who is and who was, the Holy One—because you have passed these judgments, because they poured out the blood of your saints and prophets, so you have given them blood to drink. They got what they deserved!" Then I heard the altar reply, "Yes, Lord God, the All-powerful, your judgments are true and just!" (Rev. 16:4–7)

Just when the inhabitants of the earth think their fresh water source is safe, the third bowl turns it all to blood (cf. Exod. 7:14–21). Verse 5 reflects back to God's holy purposes in the last two bowl judgments, affirming justice in that judgment. Verse 6 gives the reason for it: "because they poured out the blood of your saints and prophets," and it is followed by the pronouncement of poetic justice: "so you have given them blood to drink. They got what they deserved!" The "saints" refers to those murdered for refusing to take the mark and worshiping the Antichrist; the "prophets" likely refers to the murder of the two witnesses. In return, God will give "blood to drink" to those responsible for murder. Concluding is a reaffirmation of the power and justice of God's actions, with a voice from the altar saying, "Yes, Lord God, the All-powerful, your judgments are true and just!" (v. 7). This voice is likely the collective voice of the fifth-seal martyrs who were under the altar. "They cried out with a loud voice, "How long, Sovereign Master, holy and true, before you judge those who live on the earth and avenge our blood?" (Rev. 6:10). The term used for "true" in 6:10 and 16:7 is *alēthinos*, which refers to God's trustworthiness, i.e. faithfulness.

The fourth bowl states,

> Then the fourth angel poured out his bowl on the sun, and it was permitted to scorch people with fire. Thus people were scorched by the terrible heat, yet they blasphemed the name of God, who has ruling authority over these plagues, and they would not repent and give him glory. (Rev. 16:8–9)

This bowl judgment describes the sun causing people to be scorched with fire-heat. It shows unequivocally that the ungodly recognize these judgments as not merely being "natural" disasters; they see them as God's retribution. Fire is the basic element of wrath in the day of the Lord (e.g. Joel 2:30; Mal. 4:1; Isa. 29:6; Isa. 66:15–16; 2 Thess. 1:8; 2 Pet. 3:7; Rev. 8:5–10; 9:17–18; 11:5; 16:8–9; 18:8), including eternal judgment in hell (Rev. 14:10–11; 20:10; 21:8). The language conveys that this will be an unprecedented solar event. Regardless of how it is manifested, this judgment is reserved for punishing the wicked earth-dwellers, probably referring to those in verse 2 "who had the mark of the beast and who worshiped his image" (cf. Rev. 7:16). As a witness to their recalcitrant hearts, they "blasphemed the name of God" and thus "would not repent and give him glory." Accordingly,

God's just character is stressed again: "who has ruling authority over these plagues."

The fifth bowl states,

> Then the fifth angel poured out his bowl on the throne of the beast so that darkness covered his kingdom, and people began to bite their tongues because of their pain. They blasphemed the God of heaven because of their sufferings and because of their sores, but nevertheless they still refused to repent of their deeds. (Rev. 16:10–11)

This bowl judgment is similar to the fourth in that the recipients of God's wrath blaspheme him for punishing them for their own deeds, refusing to accept responsibility for what they, themselves, have done. This bowl judgment specifically mentions the "throne of the beast." During the great tribulation, the Antichrist exercised his authority; now his "throne" is being transferred to the kingdom of the Lord (Rev. 11:15).

It says the beast's kingdom was covered by darkness. This darkness is literal as well as symbolic, reminding the beast that he has lost control of his surroundings. The darkness in some fashion will make people begin "to bite their tongues because of their pain." This expression denotes excruciating misery. It says that one of the reasons they blaspheme God is because of their sores. This may be a carryover from the first bowl that caused sores on the beast-marked worshippers. This would suggest that the bowl judgments are not isolated; rather, their effects are cumulative.

The sixth bowl states,

> Then the sixth angel poured out his bowl on the great river Euphrates and dried up its water to prepare the way for the kings from the east. Then I saw three unclean spirits that looked like frogs coming out of the mouth of the dragon, out of the mouth of the beast, and out of the mouth of the false prophet. For

they are the spirits of the demons performing signs who go out to the kings of the earth to bring them together for the battle that will take place on the great day of God, the All-powerful. (Look! I will come like a thief! Blessed is the one who stays alert and does not lose his clothes so that he will not have to walk around naked and his shameful condition be seen.) Now the spirits gathered the kings and their armies to the place that is called Armageddon in Hebrew. (Rev. 16:12–16)

The sixth bowl is unique from the other bowl judgments because there is no expressed wrath. However, it describes the preparation for God's climactic judgment on the nations and the Antichrist at the battle of Armageddon. There is irony in this preparation. Demonic forces will draw the kings of the earth together, but the battle of Armageddon is not so much a battle as it is a divine summons for the nations to come and receive their judgment.

The sixth bowl reveals the notorious apocalyptic location where the nations' armies will gather and eventually be defeated by the Lord and his holy armies. "Now the spirits gathered the kings and their armies to the place that is called Armageddon in Hebrew" (Rev. 16:16). The New American Standard Bible renders this as "Har-magedon" (*Harmagedōn*)." The common English spelling is "Armageddon," and it is mentioned once in all of Scripture. What is the meaning of "Armageddon" (*Harmagedōn*)? In my judgment, the best understanding is in the literal sense, the Mount of Megiddo. There was a city on a hill by the name Megiddo in Palestine overlooking the Valley of Jezreel, which is also called the Valley of Megiddo. Steven Lancaster, an expert in ancient biblical geography, makes the following points.[50]

1. The Hebrew meaning of *har* does not require "mountain"; it can mean "hill." *Har* is often found in parallel with *givʿah*, which we usually translate "hill."

2. Megiddo is built upon a natural hill, and its twenty-two layers of occupation on top of the natural hill cause it to

stand up above the plain, which stretches out in front of it to the northwest, northeast, and north. The natural hill of Megiddo is one of the low hills comprising the Shephelah of Carmel, "the lowlands of Carmel"; they form an obstacle between the Sharon plain and the Jezreel Valley. In fact, its location is what made Megiddo great. It stood up and protected the most convenient pass-through, which is sometimes called the Carmel Range. Anson Rainey, the foremost historical-geographer in the study of the land of the Bible, wrote of Canaanites escaping from Pharaoh Thutmose III (who incidentally said, "capturing Megiddo is like capturing a thousand cities"): "Their escape was assured when the Egyptian troops turned aside from the pursuit to plunder the Canaanite encampments at the foot of the city's lofty mound." I quote this simply because Rainey calls the hill of Megiddo a "lofty mound," and indeed, it is. When you cross the Jezreel Valley from the north you can pick out the hill of Megiddo from miles away.

3. Zechariah 12:11 references the story of the death of King Josiah near the hill in the "Plain of Megiddo" (*biq'at Megiddon*). Yet Megiddo is not a plain either! The great site gives its name to its surroundings. Just as Megiddo gave its name to Tiglath-pileser's (III) new Assyrian province as it governed Galilee and the Jezreel plain, it gives its name to the plain that swings around it from the southeast to the northwest, and it gives its name to the hill on which it sits.

4. The term *har* is used of another city that sat above a plain. Joshua 13:19 lists among the cities of Reuben, *Tzeret ha-Shachar behar ha'emeq*, "on the hill of the plain." So the Hebrew Scriptures provide a precedent for referring to a city on a hill above a plain as related to a *har*.

5. Where did John get his Greek for *Magedon*? Megiddo occurs ten times in the Hebrew Scriptures. It does occur

in different transliterations in the LXX (Greek version of the Old Testament), but "Magedon" (*omega-nu*) is used two times when preceded by a noun: Joshua 12:21 [22 in LXX] ("the king of Magedon"); Judges 1:27 ("the inhabitants of Magedon"). The spelling "Magedon" also occurs in the Chronicles account of the death of Josiah (2 Chr. 35:22). So *har* standing before Magiddo may naturally call for *Magedon* in John's mind.

This evidence strongly supports the reference to Armageddon in Revelation 16:16 as the hill city of Megiddo and the valley it overlooks.[51]

Returning to our passage, verse 12 introduces the sixth bowl judgment by noting the first act of preparation for the great battle. The pouring out of the bowl causes the Euphrates River to dry up to prepare the way for the kings from the east. This river was the eastern boundary God gave to Israel (Gen. 15:18). Some interpreters have not taken the drying of the Euphrates literally, opting for a symbolic, spiritual truth. Yet there is nothing in the text denying a natural reading. To take it as figurative would also require the kings to be figurative, as well as the eschatological battle itself. Therefore, I see the natural sense of the narrative as prophetic, depicting a climactic battle between God and the wicked rulers of the world.

The multiplicity of kings conveys a united front. Today, the significant nations to the east of Israel are Iran, Afghanistan, Pakistan, China, and Russia. The kings from the east will cross the Euphrates, joining a coalition of other nations around the world to battle against Christ. These nations will have been pounded repeatedly by God's trumpet and bowl judgments, so thinking they can form a military coalition to put an end to Christ's new reign and divine judgments is utter foolishness.

John also sees "three unclean spirits that looked like frogs coming out of the mouth of the dragon, out of the mouth of the beast, and out of the mouth of the false prophet." The adversaries of God—the dragon, beast, and false prophet—are seen here together working in concert. The frog-like unclean spirits are demonic, performing signs for the purpose of drawing the kings of the earth to battle. The imagery reflects deception, a collaborative plot by this unholy trinity to instigate the nations to attack Christ. Later we are told, "These kings have a single intent, and they will give their power and authority to the beast. They will make war with the Lamb, but the Lamb will conquer them, because he is Lord of lords and King of kings" (Rev. 17:13–14; cf. 19:19; Psalm 110). Christ's eventual victory and subsequent rule in the earthly kingdom will cause these nations to no longer be war-driven; instead, they will be drawn to the mountain of the Lord to worship him (Isa. 2:2–4).

Finally, just before the sixth bowl concludes there is an editorial exhortation: "Look! I will come like a thief! Blessed is the one who stays alert and does not lose his clothes so that he will not have to walk around naked and his shameful condition be seen" (Rev. 16:15). Even in the midst of this apocalyptic portrayal, there is a warning to be spiritually prepared to avoid God's wrath. The book of Revelation warns us before (Rev. 1:7), during (Rev. 16:15), and after (Rev. 22:12, 20) the narrative.[52]

The seventh bowl states,

> Finally the seventh angel poured out his bowl into the air and a loud voice came out of the temple from the throne, saying: "It is done!" Then there were flashes of lightning, roaring, and crashes of thunder, and there was a tremendous earthquake—an earthquake unequaled since humanity has been on the earth, so tremendous was that earthquake. The great city was split into three parts and the cities of the nations collapsed. So Babylon the great was remembered before God, and was given the cup filled with the wine made of God's furious wrath. Every island fled away and no mountains could be found. And gigantic hailstones, weighing about a hundred pounds each, fell from heaven on people, but they blasphemed God because of the plague of hail, since it was so horrendous. (Rev. 16:17–21)

This will be the most intense expression of all the previous trumpets and bowls. The earth-dwellers will not be able to stand on the ground beneath them, nor look upward as they are pelted with immense hundred-pound hailstones. In short, the principle message sent by the final bowl is *decisiveness.*

The sixth bowl prepares for the battle of Armageddon. (For elaboration on the backdrop of the sixth and seventh bowls, see Revelation 17:1–20:3.) However, a question remains: When does the battle take place? It has often been assumed that the battle will happen during or just after the seventh bowl. I think it is more likely that it will occur just before the seventh bowl is poured out. The seventh bowl is exclusively about unprecedented catastrophes, including "an earthquake *unequaled* since humanity has been on the earth." This earthquake will decimate the entire earth, suggesting that the judgment is complete. Further, the final seventh bowl explicitly pronounces that the wrath "is done!" So I am inclined to view the final battle as taking place between the sixth and seventh bowl judgments.

When the seventh bowl is poured out, we are told, "A loud voice came out of the temple from the throne, saying, 'It is done!'" We heard this same loud voice execute the order to the angels to pour out the bowls of wrath upon the earth in the first place (cf. Rev. 16:1). The loud voice is likely from God himself as it comes from the throne. With the completion of the seventh bowl, the eschatological day of the Lord's wrath is complete. Interestingly, as Jesus was absorbing the wrath of God in the place of sinners on the cross, he said, "It is finished!" (John 19:30).

The last bowl of God's wrath begins with a storm theophany: "flashes of lightning, roaring, and crashes of thunder, and there was a tremendous earthquake—an earthquake unequaled since humanity has been on the earth." This is fitting since the wrath of God opened with a similar storm theophany introducing the trumpets (Rev. 8:5), including a similar one at the seventh trumpet (Rev. 11:19). Given the similarities between the seventh-bowl earthquake and the previous ones, one might assume that it is one and the same. However, the seventh-bowl earthquake cannot be identified with the previous earthquakes depicted in the book of Revelation for three main reasons: (1) the bowls are not a restatement or summary of the trumpets; they function as their own set of judgments, progressively becoming *intensified*; (2) John the apostle, who penned Revelation, goes out of his way to highlight the unprecedented nature of the seventh-bowl earthquake ("There was a tremendous earthquake—an earthquake unequaled since humanity has been on the earth, so tremendous was that earthquake") ; and (3) it is associated with the pronouncement, "It is done!"

This massive earthquake will also have a very specific purpose on a city: "The great city was split into three parts and the cities of the nations collapsed." There is debate on the identity of the great city (Rev. 11:8). In my estimation, Jerusalem is the most plausible referent based on the clause "where their Lord was also crucified." To be sure, the great city is not present-day Jerusalem, but the *eschatological* city of Jerusalem. The term for "nations" in the expression "the cities of the nations collapsed" is *ethnos*, which can mean "Gentiles." In this specific context, the Jewish "great city" is contrasted with the cities in Gentile nations. This city is also identified as Babylon. "A second angel followed the first, declaring: 'Fallen, fallen is Babylon the great city! She made all the nations drink of the wine of her immoral passion'" (Rev. 14:8; cf. 17:2). In our seventh-bowl passage it states, "So Babylon the great was remembered before God, and was given the cup filled with the wine made of God's furious wrath" (Rev. 16:19). As Babylon made the nations "drink of the wine" of her immorality, now God makes Babylon drink of the wine of his "furious wrath" (cf. Rev. 18:5–6). There is additional support identifying "Babylon the Great" as the eschatological city of Jerusalem; but it is not my purpose to discuss the rise and fall of this city and the nations under the beast's kingdom as described in the parenthesis in Revelation 17:1–20:3. I refer the reader to further study on this topic.[53]

Returning to the global effect of the unprecedented earthquake, the following is a sober pronouncement: "Every island fled away and no mountains could be found." Mountains connote strength and immovableness, but the one who created them will cause them to be no more, however that will happen. At the moment the earth loses all stability, the sky turns chaotic with "gigantic hailstones, weighing about a hundred pounds each, [falling] from heaven on people." The ungodly not only refuse to repent, but they "blasphemed God because of the plague of hail, since it was so horrendous" (Rev. 16:21; cf. Exod. 9:23–25; Ezek. 38:22). They foolishly blame God for their misery.

Post Seven-Year Period

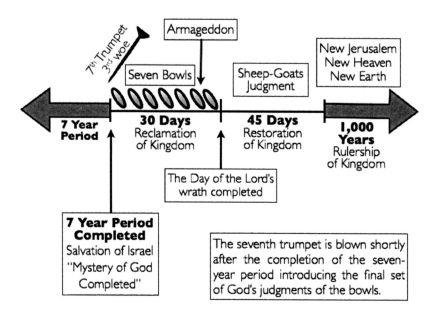

Conclusion

In Part 3, I started with explaining the expression "the day of the Lord." Then I considered the day of the Lord that Jesus knew from the Jewish prophets, followed by Jesus' teaching that the rapture will happen on the same day that the day of the Lord's wrath begins. Next I focused on the apostle Paul's teaching of the day of the Lord, concluding with the book of Revelation's portrayal of the systematic judgments. For my final thoughts, see the Epilogue.

Epilogue

In Luke 18:8 Jesus asks the question, "When the Son of Man comes, will he find faith on earth?" Jesus' ominous question to us all implies that there will be a temptation to apostatize. In his Olivet Discourse, Jesus warns that there will be concrete temptations facing believers during the great tribulation, including persecution, deception, and slothfulness. It is imperative that we prepare our hearts to be "overcomers" for what may soon come to pass. This is why Jesus warns, "Remember, I have told you ahead of time" (Matt. 24:25).

Besides exhorting his people to have faith in light of his return, there are at least three purposes served by the doctrine of the second coming in our daily lives—sanctification, evangelism, and peace in God's sovereignty.

First, it is an act of love that God reveals to us this prophetic truth because he seeks to sanctify us through it. The certainty of God's judgment is sobering. In light of the day of the Lord's judgment, Peter asks, "What sort of people must we be, conducting our lives in holiness and godliness, while waiting for and hastening the coming of the day of God?" (2 Pet. 3:11–12). Thus, the doctrine of the second coming induces us to search our hearts for any worldly attachments lest they be exposed at the revelation of Christ. As we wait for either death or the second coming, the Lord instructs us to live in godly ways in order to emerge victorious at his return.

> "If anyone wants to become my follower, he must deny himself, take up his cross, and follow me. For whoever wants to save his life will lose it, but whoever loses his life for my sake will find it. For what does it benefit a person if he gains the whole world but forfeits his life? Or what can a person give in exchange for his life? For the Son of Man will come with his angels in the glory of his Father, and then he will reward each person according to what he has done." (Matt. 16:24–27)

Second, this biblical truth should propel us to proclaim the gospel to the lost world. The Lord has not returned because the fullness of his elect continues to be drawn in through repentance and faith. "The Lord is not slow concerning his promise, as some regard slowness, but is being patient toward you, because he does not wish for any to perish but for all to come to repentance" (2 Pet. 3:9). And the apostle Paul writes, "Consequently faith comes from what is heard, and what is heard comes through the preached word of Christ" (Rom. 10:17). The motivation for evangelizing the lost is the *certainty* of the Lord's return and the *consequences* for unbelievers unprepared to meet the Lord.

Third, this biblical truth reminds us that God, not Satan, is sovereign. God will seek to glorify himself through upholding his righteousness and vindicating his people in the judgment of his enemies. The day of the Lord's judgment is the transitional phase into the day of the Lord's peace. It will usher in his majesty when his name is exalted and the nations say, "Come on! Let's go up to the Lord's mountain, to the temple of Jacob's God, so he can teach us his commands and we can live by his laws" (Micah 4:2).

God's plan is flawless. There are no purposeless tragedies in his sovereign creation. God has decreed the end as well as the means, and he will be glorified for his all-wise, free-mercy, and holy-just actions. This includes our salvation, for none of us will be standing before the throne of God saying, "I am the reason why I am here." No! We will all be giving the Almighty God *all* the glory (Rev. 7:9–17; Rev. 15:1–4).

Appendix 1.
Key Terms Related to the Return of Christ

The Meaning of *Parousia*

The Greek noun for "coming" is *parousia*, which means "an arrival and a continuing presence." It is the word used in the disciples' question in Matthew 24:3, and it is the term behind the theological expression "second coming" or "second advent." In the New Testament, it is always in the singular, not the plural, and is used twenty-four times.[54] Seventeen times it is used prophetically of our Lord's second coming, including four instances in Matthew 24 (the only instances recorded in all four gospels). In secular Greek, it was commonly used to refer to a king's royal visit to another land. It is befitting that Matthew applies this term to Christ's return since there is a royal motif in the book, portraying Jesus' inaugural fulfillment as the Davidic King. *Parousia* can also carry the sense, "the coming of a hidden divinity, who makes his presence felt by a revelation of his power." Jesus will manifest himself when he returns, making his presence felt through the revelation of the day-of-the-Lord judgments. Believers are told to make Jesus' parousia the object of expectation (1 Thess. 2:19; 3:13; 4:15; 5:23; 2 Thess. 2:1, 8; James 5:7–8; 2 Pet. 3:12; 1 John 2:28).

The Lord's second coming (*parousia*) will be a comprehensive-complex whole. It will not be a simple, instantaneous event as the rapture will be. The scope will include various events that will fulfill divine purposes. This is consistent with Jesus' first coming. When we think of his first coming, we do not think exclusively of his birth. Indeed, his birth was his "arrival," but his subsequent "presence" included his upbringing, teaching ministry, miracles, discipling, death, burial, and resurrection. It was a comprehensive-complex whole that God used to fulfill his purposes. Similarly, the second coming will begin with Jesus' arrival in the clouds to resurrect the dead and rapture them along with believers who are still alive at that time (1 Thess. 4:13–18). The biblical writers often emphasized the arrival aspect of the parousia because they wanted to induce godly living in their listeners. But it would be a mistake to think they viewed the parousia as limited only to his glorious appearing in the sky resulting in the resurrection of the dead and the rapture. His *subsequent* presence will encompass major events such as the day of the Lord's wrath, bringing the remnant of Israel to salvation, and reclaiming his earthly regal-rule that will extend through the millennium. In short, Christ is coming back as deliverer, judge, and king. Paul shows a specific relationship between the parousia and the kingdom:

> But each in his own order: Christ, the firstfruits; then when Christ comes [*parousia*], those who belong to him. Then comes the end, when he hands over the kingdom to God the Father, when he has brought to an end all rule and all authority and power. For he must reign until he has put all his enemies under his feet. The last enemy to be eliminated is death. For he has put everything in subjection under his feet. But when it says "everything" has been put in subjection, it is clear that this does not include the one who put everything in subjection to him. And when all things are subjected to him, then the Son himself will be subjected to the one who subjected everything to him, so that God may be all in all. (1 Cor. 15:23–28)

Paul states that when the series of resurrections is accomplished, Christ will "reign until" all his enemies, especially death, are defeated. He will hand over the kingdom to God the Father when everything is put into subjection. Paul teaches that the first divine purpose of the parousia will be the resurrection. After the day of the Lord's judgment, the parousia will extend into his rule in the physical glorified kingdom, eventuating in all enemies being eliminated. Accordingly, his parousia will not be an instantaneous event; it will be a multi-phased, complex-whole in which God will fulfill his divine purposes: "Then the Son himself will be subjected to the one who subjected everything to him, so that God may be all in all."

There is one last point to be made about the word *parousia*. The term is co-referential with the expression "the day of the Lord." These are not two separate events, but one and the same. However, each expression can have its own nuance depending on the context: the day of the Lord expressing generally a negative-judgment aspect of our Lord's return and parousia expressing a generally positive-redemptive aspect of our Lord's return. Both Peter and Paul understood these terms to be co-referential.

> But the *day of the Lord* will come like a thief; when it comes, the heavens will disappear with a horrific noise, and the celestial bodies will melt away in a blaze, and the earth and every deed done on it will be laid bare. Since all these things are to melt away in this manner, what sort of people must we be, conducting our lives in holiness and godliness, while waiting for and hastening the *coming* [parousia] of the day of God? Because of this day, the heavens will be burned up and dissolve, and the celestial bodies will melt away in a blaze! (2 Pet. 3:10–12, emphasis mine)

He will also strengthen you to the end, so that you will be blameless on the *day of our Lord Jesus Christ* (1 Cor. 1:8). So that your hearts are strengthened in holiness to be blameless before our God and Father at the *coming* [parousia] of our

Lord Jesus with all his saints (1 Thess. 3:13, emphasis mine; cf. 5:23).[55]

Parousia/Day of the Lord's Arrival and Continued Presence

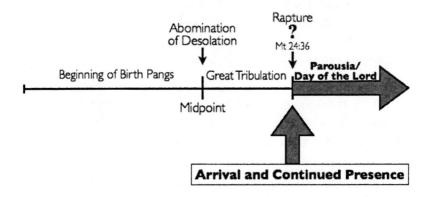

The Meaning of *Apokalypsis*

In 2 Thessalonians 1:7, the persecuted church is instructed to wait for relief that will come at Christ's "revelation," or *apokalypsis*, a word meaning "making fully known, revelation, disclosure." Paul uses this term elsewhere. For example, he says we should wait for it "so that you do not lack any spiritual gift as you wait for the revelation [*apokalypsis*] of our Lord Jesus Christ" (1 Cor. 1:7; cf. 1 Pet 1:7, 13; 4:13; Rom. 8:19; see also the verb form *apokalyptō* in Luke 17:30; Rom. 8:18; 1 Cor. 3:13). In the very next verse, Paul equates the revelation with the day of the Lord. "He will also strengthen you to the end, so that you will be blameless on the day of our Lord Jesus Christ" (1 Cor. 1:8).

Relief and Judgment at the *Apokalypsis*

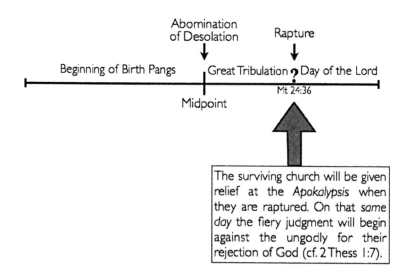

The surviving church will be given relief at the *Apokalypsis* when they are raptured. On that *same day* the fiery judgment will begin against the ungodly for their rejection of God (cf. 2 Thess 1:7).

A question remains: What is disclosed or veiled at this time that will later be revealed? Since theophanies are mostly revelations, we can ask, what is God revealing about his will? A physical-visionary revelation is not contrary to an intellectual-knowledge revelation. Both will be present at the revelation of Christ. In fact, it can be understood that through the physical-visionary, the Lord can reveal his divine will to serve a twofold purpose: one for the godly and one for the ungodly.

Visionary: 'The Lord Jesus is Revealed from Heaven'
God's will for the godly: "to give rest"
God's will for the ungodly: "mete out punishment"

The Meaning of *Phaneroō, Epiphaneia, Epiphanēs*

The next term is the verb "to appear," *phaneroō*, meaning "to cause to become visible, reveal, expose publicly." This term contains an emphasis on the sensory rather than the cognitive. When Scripture uses this term in the context of the second coming, it refers to the appearing of Christ at the initiation of his parousia. For example, the apostle John exhorts believers to abide in Christ until he comes back. "And now, little children, remain in him, so that when he appears [*phaneroō*] we may have confidence and not shrink away from him in shame when he comes back [*parousia*]" (1 John 2:28; cf. 1 John 3:2; Col. 3:4; 1 Pet. 5:4).

There is also the noun form "appearing," *epiphaneia*, which means "an act of appearing, appearance." It has the connotation of a *splendid* manifestation. In the first-century Greek world, this was a term as it related to transcendence in the sense of a "sudden manifestation of a hidden divinity, either in the form of a personal appearance, or by some deed of power or oracular communication by which its presence is made known." In Paul's exhortation to Timothy to fight the good fight of the faith and pursue righteousness, he orders him, "[O]bey this command without fault or failure until the appearing [*epiphaneia*] of our Lord Jesus Christ" (1 Tim. 6:14). To Titus, he says, ". . . as we wait for the happy fulfillment of our hope in the glorious appearing [*epiphaneia*] of our great God and Savior, Jesus Christ" (Titus 2:13; cf. 2 Tim. 4:1, 8).

The use of this term by the apostle Paul has ramifications for pretribulationism. As shown in the verses above, Paul teaches that the church will be here until the "appearing" of Christ, or as some translations render it, "manifestation." He also instructs that the Antichrist will be present at the appearing-manifestation of our Lord: "and then the lawless one [i.e. the Antichrist] will be revealed, whom the Lord will destroy by the breath of his mouth and wipe out by the manifestation [*epiphaneia*] of his arrival" (2 Thess. 2:8). The inference is clear: The Antichrist will first be revealed, then at a later time Christ will be revealed. Thus, both the church and the Antichrist will be present together on earth when Christ comes back. To claim, as pretribulationists do, that the Antichrist will be revealed after Christ is revealed turns Paul's explicit statement on its head. Both the church and the Antichrist will exist on earth when Christ is revealed. When Christ is revealed, the church will be delivered out of the hands of the Antichrist.

Finally, the adjective form "glorious," *epiphanēs*, is employed by Luke to contrast the dark celestial disturbances. "The sun will be changed to darkness and the moon to blood before the great and glorious [*epiphanēs*] day of the Lord comes" (Acts 2:20).

This rich vocabulary describes the unique and awesome event of our Lord's return. The term *parousia* highlights the regal-presence of Christ. The *apokalypsis* depicts the full knowledge-disclosure of Christ. The word group *phaneroō, epiphaneia,* and *epiphanēs* describe the dazzling glory-manifestation of Christ. These actions portray, not disconnected events, but complementary actions, providing a stunning, glorious portrayal of Jesus' return.

Appendix 2.
Parallels between Jesus and Paul

T here are thirty parallels between Jesus' teaching on the second coming in the Olivet Discourse and Paul's teaching on the second coming in the Thessalonian letters. This comparison of Scripture with Scripture shows Paul's dependence on the Olivet Discourse. We should not be surprised by these parallels since Paul explicitly claims dependence on Jesus: "by the word of the Lord" (1 Thess. 4:15). This demonstrates that Jesus intended the Olivet Discourse to be a teaching for *the church*. It is profoundly mistaken to dismiss Jesus' warnings in the Olivet Discourse for the church today, making them applicable only to believers in A.D. 70 (preterism) or to Jewish believers during the tribulation (pretribulationism).

Jesus Matt. 24–25	Parallels on the Second Coming	Paul I & II Thess.
24:3–4	Christ is the Source	I.4:15
24:3, 27, 37, 39	Context: The Parousia	I.4:15; II.2:1, 8
24:4–5, 23–26	Do Not Be Deceived	II.2:3
24:6	Alarmed the End Has Come	II.2:2
24:15	Antichrist's Desolation	II.2.4
24:21–22	Opposition By Antichrist	II.2:3–4, 8–9
24:24	Deceiving Signs and Wonders	II.2:9–10
24:24	Elect Will Not Be Deceived	II.2:9–14
24:12	Lawlessness	II.2:3, 12
24:10–11	Apostasy of Many	II.2:3
24:13, 22, 31, 40–41 (Lk 21:28)	Surviving Believers Delivered	I.4:15, 17; 5:9; II.1:7
24:22, 29–31	Persecution Cut Short	II.1:6–7; 2:8
24:27, 30	Initiation of the Parousia	I.4:15, II.2:1, 8
24:29–30	Parousia Follows Antichrist	II.2:8
24:27–30	Universal Perception	I.4:16; II.1:7–8
24:30	Jesus with Clouds	I.4:17
24:30	Power and Glory	II.1:9
24:31	Angelic Presence	I.4:16; II.1:7
24:31	Trumpet Call	I.4:16
24:31	Gathering	I.4:17; II.2:1
25:6	Meeting (*Apantēsis*)	I.4:17
24:37–41 (Lk 17:22–35)	Back-to-Back Rapture & Wrath	II.1:6–10
24:37–41	"Peace and Safety"	I.5:3
24:43	Thief in the Night	I.5:2, 4
24:37–41 (Lk 21:34)	Sudden Destruction for Ungodly	I.5:2–3
24:29–30, 37–39	Initiation of the Day of the Lord	I.5:1–3, II.1:7–8
25:10–13 (Lk 21:36)	Inescapable for the Unprepared	I.5:3
24:32–33	Knowing the Season	I.5:1
24:45–46	The Faithful at His Coming	I.5:4–5, 8
24:42–25:13 (Lk 21:34–36)	Be Watchful and Expectant	I.5:6–8

Some object to prewrath by pointing out that there are elements "lacking" in either Jesus' or Paul's teaching and therefore they cannot be referring to the same event. For example, they will state that Paul never mentions the celestial disturbances found in Jesus' account; therefore, Paul cannot be speaking about the same coming Jesus teaches. This type of argumentation is unreasonable, demanding that when a New Testament writer teaches on a doctrine he must be exhaustive in every element of it. Incidentally, Paul does refer to the celestial-disturbance event indirectly. In 1 Thessalonians 5:3, his statement, "Sudden destruction comes on them, like labor pains on a pregnant woman, and they will surely not escape" is drawn from Isaiah 13:6–10, which is a prominent celestial-disturbance passage!

Pretribulationists and preterists would never be this unreasonable with other doctrines containing this many parallels. What if we applied their skeptical standard to doctrines such as the deity of Christ or salvation? We could never draw any conclusions if every passage on a doctrinal topic was required to contain virtually the same elements as every other passage. Imagine if we applied this standard to studying the gospel stories! There would be no reason to possess four gospel accounts because we would need only one. God ordained four portraits on the life of Jesus, with each gospel writer giving a different perspective complementing the others (e.g. genealogies, the birth of Jesus, the Lord's prayer, the Gadarene demoniacs, the crucifixion, and the resurrection). Accordingly, it is correct to view Jesus' and Paul's teaching on the second coming, not as incompatible, but as complementary and harmonious.

Another objection pretribulationists and preterists cite is that a reference to a "multitude" of angels is lacking in Paul's rapture passage in 1 Thessalonians 4:13–18. Paul mentions only an archangel, while Jesus references a multitude of angels. Again, we should not be selective with the evidence because we need to include Paul's entire eschatological Thessalonian teaching on Christ's coming. In his second Thessalonian epistle, he taught that Jesus will give relief to his persecuted church when "angels" (plural) accompany him at his return: "and to you who are being afflicted to give rest together with us when the Lord Jesus is revealed from heaven with his mighty *angels*" (2 Thess. 1:7, emphasis mine). Further, we know from Luke 9:26 that a host of angels will accompany Christ when he comes back for his church. "For whoever is ashamed of me and my words, the Son of Man will be ashamed of that person when he comes in his glory and in the glory of the Father and of the holy angels." Instead of these two accounts being incompatible, they are consistent.

One last objection I will mention claims that the teachings of Jesus and Paul contradict one another; hence it is argued that they must be addressing two different subjects. For example, it is contended that in Matthew 24 angels do the gathering, while in Paul's teaching the Lord himself gathers. But this is not a contradiction since Paul never states that the Lord himself gathers. The verb in 1 Thessalonians 4:17 "will be suddenly caught up" (*harpagēsometha*) is in the passive voice, with an *unstated* subject doing the action. Believers will meet the Lord in the sky, but the agent who actually gathers them is left unstated. It is reading into the text to assume that the Lord himself is the primary agent who does the gathering. Moreover, even if the text had said that Jesus gathered believers to himself, it would not rule out angels being used as his instrument to do so. For example, the Bible speaks about the Lord pouring out his wrath when he comes back (e.g. Rev. 6:16–17), yet we know that Jesus will use angels as the instruments to execute his judgments (e.g. Matt. 13:41; 2 Thess. 1:7; Rev. 8–9; Rev. 14:15–19; Rev. 15–16).

In summary, Jesus' teaching and Paul's teaching on the second coming complement each other, giving a consistent picture. The overwhelming parallels between their accounts show they are clearly speaking of the same future second coming of our Lord.

Appendix 3.
Proposed Structure to the Book of Revelation

If the book of Revelation did not exist, we would still possess an abundance of material concerning God's eschatological day of judgment through the Old Testament prophets, Jesus' teaching, and Paul's epistles. But we should be thankful for the book of Revelation because it gives us a detailed and systematic account of the outpouring of God's wrath via the trumpet and bowl judgments, developing a richer picture of the day of the Lord. This systematic-judgment phenomenon is not new in Scripture; for example, God systematically intensified the plagues upon Egypt (Exod. 7–12). The very first kingdom to persecute God's people, Egypt, experienced God's systematic wrath; likewise, the very last kingdom to persecute God's people, the Antichrist's kingdom, also will be subjected to God's systematic wrath.

The "John" mentioned in Revelation 1:1 is most likely the apostle John. He wrote in the genre of predictive-eschatology, written as an epistle, which was a circular letter to seven churches in Asia Minor written about A.D. 95.

There have generally been two major areas of disagreement among Christians on how to approach the book of Revelation.

First, are the events it portrays to be interpreted in a literal historical fashion? Or were they intended to be interpreted symbolically—as timeless, ethical or spiritual truths about the struggle between good and evil (idealism)? If they describe literal historical events, were these events fulfilled in the first century (preterism)? Are they unfolding throughout church history (historicism)? Or will they largely be played out in the future in relation to the return of Christ (futurism)?

I will use the Antichrist event to illustrate these different approaches. Revelation 13 depicts an antichrist figure. Should we interpret this figure as *only* symbolizing evil attempting to thwart God's purposes for his church (idealism)? Or is this a referent to a historical figure in the first century, such as Nero or Domitian (preterism)? Shall we understand this antichrist figure as being personified in the papacy, dictatorial government, or some other institution throughout history (historicism)? Or should the antichrist referent be viewed as a real person to emerge in the future who will oppose God's people just before Christ returns (futurism)?

Over time, Christians have held all four of these views. The position taken in this book is the futurist interpretation. This is not to say that believers in John's day were not experiencing trials resembling those prophetically described in Revelation; and certainly there are timeless, spiritual truths contained in the book, instructing every generation of the church. However, these latter purposes should not eclipse the message of eschatological persecution of the church by the Antichrist and the exhortations to believers to persevere (*hypomonē*), overcome (*nikaō*), hear (*akouō*), and have faith (*pistis*). Since I am writing for futurists, it is not necessary to spend the time establishing the futurist approach. However, for those interested in that debate, I refer the reader to some helpful literature.[56]

A second area of disagreement with respect to the book of Revelation is the structure of the book. There is, however, consensus on a basic formal structure. Most agree that the prologue is found in Revelation 1:1–8 or 1:1–20 and the epilogue in 22:6–21. There is also widespread agreement that the letters to the seven churches in chapters 2–3 contain a discernible section. So we are left with the body in Revelation 4:1–22:5. There have been several valid proposals regarding its structure.

Some have structured it by seeing a *temporal* nature from John's perspective. "Therefore write what you saw, what is, and what will be after these things" (Rev. 1:19).[57] Another common arrangement is the *literary* nature in which John is summoned three times to witness sets of new visions (4:1–16:21; 17:1–21:8; 21:9–22:5). Some prefer to view Revelation principally through the lens of a *kingdom* division in which the first half (1–11) narrates events unfolding up to God's reclamation of his kingdom and defeat of Satan's: "The kingdom of the world has become the kingdom of our Lord and of his Christ, and he will reign for ever and ever" (Rev. 11:15). The second half (12–22) is understood as restating these events by expanding or fleshing them out. Finally, the most conspicuous structure John gives is the *septet* (set of seven) arrangement, with five series of sevens, or septets. The first septet is the letters to the seven churches (2–3). The second is a scroll sealed with seven seals (6:1–17; 8:1). The third is the trumpet judgments (8:2–9:21; 11:15–19). The fourth is the bowls, which are said to contain God's final wrath (15:1–16:21). The fifth septet—the only one not explicitly enumerated—is seven visions that share similar features with each other (12–14).

Another literary phenomenon in the book that is very important but sometimes minimized is the use of parentheses. Parentheses function as pauses in the narrative to provide development on previous events before moving on again. There are minor parenthetical passages scattered throughout the book and two major parenthetical passages (12–14; 17:1–20:3). The first half of the book, chapters 1–11, is naturally sequential, taking us up to the completion of the seven-year period. Following this is the first major parenthetical section in chapters 12–14, giving a panoramic view of the kingdom conflict between Satan and God. The section spans the period of the Messianic promise during Israel's history, then focuses mostly on the Antichrist's great tribulation and concludes with the eschatological harvests of deliverance and judgment at Christ's coming.[58] The narrative picks up at Revelation 15–16 with the bowl judgments. The second major parenthetical section is found in chapters 17:1–20:3. This section develops a few key events, including the sixth and seventh bowls, the great prostitute and the beast's authority, the destruction of the great city of "Babylon," God being glorified from heaven, the marriage supper of the Lamb, and the defeat of the "three adversaries of God." Finally, the conclusion to the book highlights the beginning of the millennium in chapters 20:4–22:21.

I want to make a couple of remarks about the first major parenthetical section found in Revelation 12–14 so we might properly interpret it in light of the overall structure in the book. First, we cannot force every chapter into a chronological fashion; otherwise, we will find ourselves confounded by conflicting events, especially with the events described in this section. To be sure, the narrative does exhibit a *general-progressive* movement. For example, we know that the climax in chapters 19–22 follows the narrative in Revelation in chapters 1–18; and it is self-evident that chapters 6–22 follow chapters 1–5. Even though the narrative chapters of the seals, trumpets, and bowls are sequential, chapters 12–14 are peculiar in that they do not chronologically follow the narrative in chapters 8–11. For example, references in chapters 12–14 depict the beginning of the Antichrist's campaign, while the narrative in chapters 8–9 describes the trumpet judgments. But we know that God's wrath does not begin *before* the persecution of the Antichrist. So how does the interpreter account for this exception to an otherwise sequential narrative? The question of the chronology of chapters 12–14 is resolved when interpreters recognize that these chapters function as a parenthetical unit containing seven visions. They serve to pause the narrative to give development on previous events that happened mostly during the seven-year period before picking up again in chapters 15–16, which describe the bowl judgments that will occur immediately after the seven-year period.

The literary device of parentheses is not unique to Revelation. It is also found in two other eschatological passages: Matthew 24 and Daniel 7. Matthew 24:9–14 is an overview of the great tribulation, while verses 15–28 are parenthetical, developing the great tribulation. Daniel 7:1–14 is a narrative overview followed by a parenthetical development of the fourth beast in verses 15–27. A "forest picture" of the book of Revelation will be helpful since it is easy to become lost within the trees of the verses.

Here is my proposed structure to the book of Revelation.

PROLOGUE AND RECIPIENTS
1. Prologue
2–3. The Seven Churches

BEFORE THE DAY OF THE LORD
4. A Vision of Heavenly Worship
5. The Seven-Sealed Scroll and the Worthy Lamb
6. Opening the Six Seals
7. Protected: 144,000 Jews Sealed and an Innumerable Multitude Delivered

THE DAY OF THE LORD
8. Seventh Seal Opened: First Four Trumpet Judgments
9. Fifth Trumpet / First Woe; Sixth Trumpet / Second Woe

SEVEN-YEAR PERIOD COMPLETED
10. Mighty Angel and the Mystery of God Completed
11:1–13. Completion of Ministry of the Two Witnesses
11:14–19. Seventh Trumpet / Third Woe and God's Kingdom Reclaimed

PARENTHESIS 1: COSMIC CONFLICT
12. Panorama of Satan's Schemes
13. Loyalty to the Antichrist or Jesus Christ?
14. Redeemed 144,000 Jews; Impending Judgments; Harvests of the Earth

THE DAY OF THE LORD COMPLETED

15. Prelude to the Bowl Judgments
16. Seventh Trumpet / Third Woe Continued in the Seven Bowl Judgments

PARENTHESIS 2: THE FALL OF BABYLON AND ANTICHRIST

17. The Great Prostitute and the Beast's Authority
18. Destruction of the Great City of "Babylon"
19:1–10. God Glorified from Heaven; Marriage Supper of the Lamb
19:11–20:3. Defeat of the "Three Adversaries of God"

BEGINNING OF THE MILLENNIUM AND RENEWAL

20:4–6. Types of Resurrection
20:7–15. Satan and the Ungodly Perish
21:1–22:5. New Heaven, New Earth, New Jerusalem
22:6–21. Epilogue

Appendix 4.
Expectancy, Not Imminency

Since the day of the Lord's wrath begins on the very same day that God delivers the righteous (Luke 17:22–35; 2 Thess. 1:6–10), this has ramifications for the pretribulational teaching that Christ can rapture the church at any moment (i.e. imminency). Imminency means that there cannot be any prophesied events that *must* occur before the rapture. Pretribulationists argue that if the Bible predicts an event happening before the rapture, then Christ's return can no longer be imminent. But does the Bible teach imminency? Scripture gives four explicit prophesied events that must occur before the day of the Lord. Given this same-day teaching of rapture and wrath, by necessity these events will occur before the rapture. We have already discussed the celestial disturbance event, but it would be good to note it again here.

> "I will produce portents both in the sky and on the earth—blood, fire, and columns of smoke. The sunlight will be turned to darkness and the moon to the color of blood, before the day of the Lord comes—that great and terrible day!" (Joel 2:30–31)

A second Old Testament prophet, Malachi, foretold another event that would take place before the day of the Lord. "Look, I will send you Elijah the prophet *before* the great and terrible day of the Lord arrives" (Mal. 4:5, emphasis mine). John the Baptist was a type or pattern of Elijah, but he was not the fulfillment of his ministry.[59]

Turning to the New Testament, we see that the apostle Paul furnishes us with two more prophetic events that will occur before the day of the Lord (and thereby before the rapture). He writes,

> Now concerning the coming of our Lord Jesus Christ and our being gathered together to him, we ask you, brothers, not to be quickly shaken in mind or alarmed, either by a spirit or a spoken word, or a letter seeming to be from us, to the effect that the day of the Lord has come. Let no one deceive you in any way. For that day will not come, unless the rebellion comes first, and the man of lawlessness is revealed, the son of destruction, who opposes and exalts himself against every so-called god or object of worship, so that he takes his seat in the temple of God, proclaiming himself to be God. (2 Thess. 2:1–4 ESV)

In this passage, it is noteworthy that Paul gives the rapture ("gathered together to him") a close connection to the day of the Lord. He does this because in the immediate context, he explains that the wrath of God begins on the same day as God's people are delivered from their persecution (2 Thess. 1:6–10). Then he gives two discernible events that must occur before the day of the Lord begins, reassuring the Thessalonian believers that the day of the Lord's wrath has not yet occurred: (1) "the rebellion" (i.e. a well-known apostasy that will take place) and (2) the "man of lawlessness" (i.e. the Antichrist) will be revealed, who will take "his seat in the temple of God, proclaiming himself to be God."

Instead of imminency, the Bible teaches *expectancy* for our Lord's return. The New Testament writers address their contemporary believers as if the second coming of Christ could happen in their generation, but not before key prophetic events—the celestial disturbances, the coming of Elijah, the apostasy, and the Antichrist's revelation— would take place.[60] It is possible that our generation of the church could be the one that witnesses these events. Time will tell. In the meantime, we must be watchful, obedient, and faithful to our Lord, lest he comes back at a time we are not spiritually ready to meet him.

Expectancy—Not Imminency

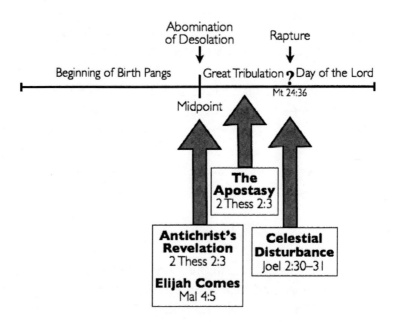

Next, I want to briefly respond to the pretribulational proof text of Titus 2:13: "waiting for our blessed hope, the appearing of the glory of our great God and Savior Jesus Christ" (ESV). This verse is used as a proof text, but it contains no hint of imminency. The verse simply teaches that our blessed hope is the "appearing of the glory of our great God and Savior Jesus Christ." Pretribulationism teaches that the return of Jesus can no longer be a blessed hope if prophetic events must occur before the rapture. But why not? Logically, that makes no sense. I can look forward to the blessed time when the spring flowers bloom, but before that happens the snow must first melt. And I can look forward to being a parent, but a couple of things must happen first unless a stork imminently comes along! Saying that the rapture cannot be a blessed hope if there are prophesied events that must come first makes no biblical sense either. For example, Peter writes,

> Since all these things are thus to be dissolved, what sort of people ought you to be in lives of holiness and godliness, waiting for and hastening the coming of the day of God, because of which the heavens will be set on fire and dissolved, and the heavenly bodies will melt as they burn! But according to his promise we are waiting for new heavens and a new earth in which righteousness dwells. (2 Pet. 3:11–13 ESV)

Peter teaches that we are to wait for the blessed time of the new heavens and new earth, for it is a "promise" when "righteousness dwells." At the same time we long for that blessed age, Peter describes the coming of the day of God's wrath that must happen *before* that blessed time. Thus there is biblical precedent to long for a blessed time, even though it will be preceded by other events. Moreover, the term for "waiting" in Titus 2:13 ("waiting for our blessed hope") is *prosdechomai,* which simply means "look forward to the fulfillment of our expectation." The term never means "imminence."[61]

Another objection I have heard not a few times is that the blessed hope cannot be blessed if the church has to go through the Antichrist's great tribulation before the rapture. A version of this goes something like: "I am looking for the true Christ, not the Antichrist!" This sounds pious at first, but there is no biblical substance behind it. In contrast, Peter instructs the church that persecution will be the norm occurring right up to the return of Christ.

> Beloved, do not be surprised at the fiery trial when it comes upon you to test you, as though something strange were happening to you. But rejoice insofar as you share Christ's suffer-

ings, that you may also rejoice and be glad when his glory is revealed. (1 Pet. 4:12–13 ESV)

Not only does Peter teach that the revelation of Christ will be a time of rejoicing, but he teaches that the persecution that occurs just beforehand will make that return *all the more* blessed. For Peter, knowing difficult times are coming should intensify our blessed hope to be with the Lord, not diminish it. In short, Peter and Paul speak of the *doxa*, the glory, of his revelation/appearing, which will be a time of blessed rejoicing.

Here is something else to consider. For which group of believers do you think the return of Christ will be considered more blessed: complacent believers fixed on their couches, watching television and filling their stomachs full of food, or believers who live in a persecuted country fasting and trusting God during the threat of imprisonment? I think the answer is obvious. The Antichrist's great tribulation will refine the faith of believers and galvanize eager anticipation to be with their Rescuer-Groom. The blessed hope is not a secret, imminent rapture. It is simply seeing and being with our Savior in our glorified state at his revelation. The great tribulation will heighten that hope.

Pretribulational imminency is a relatively new British-American teaching in church history, originating in the nineteenth century by the Plymouth Brethren theologian John Nelson Darby. If it is found in other parts of the world today, it is only because it has been exported by American and British pretribulational missionaries. This teaching may sound new, even challenging to some readers. You might have grown up in a tradition that assumed the imminency of the Lord's return. If this describes you, I encourage you to be a "Berean" in the faith and test everything with the Word of God. "These [Bereans] were more open-minded than those in Thessalonica, for they eagerly received the message, examining the scriptures carefully every day to see if these things were so" (Acts 17:11).

Appendix 5.
What Did the Early Church Believe?

The development of prewrath eschatology in recent decades has refined our theological understanding of the day of the Lord and the rapture.[62] The essence of prewrath teaching, however, reaches back to the early church period, finding testimony even in the first century in the earliest Christian document outside the New Testament. This document is called the Didache, "the Teaching" (a.k.a. *The Teaching of the Twelve Apostles*), pronounced DID-ah-kay. By the essence of the prewrath position, I mean specifically the teaching that the church will encounter the persecution of the Antichrist, followed by the coming of Christ to rescue and resurrect his people.

The Didache is an extremely important early Christian document because it is a window allowing us to see the faith and practice of a segment of the primitive church. Dated between A.D. 50–120, it is a compositional document of several sources, the earliest written likely before A.D. 70. The probable place of origin is Syria, perhaps in the city of Antioch, the main Christian center at the time. The Didache is made up of three parts. The first is a code of Christian morals, the "Two Ways," which expounds on the way of life and the way of death. The second is a church order manual of rules of conduct prescribing the correct practice of baptism, church polity, the Lord's Supper, and other matters. It concludes with an eschatological section giving a commentary outlining Matthew's Olivet Discourse. The Didache is the first interpretation in recorded church history of Jesus' teaching about his second coming.

The early church embraced the Didache as containing orthodox teaching, including its interpretation of eschatology. This document was so important that it led some early church fathers (albeit wrongly) to accept it as Scripture. But mainly it was used for instruction for church leaders, believers, and baptismal candidates. The eschatological section of the Didache is found in chapter 16.

> (1) Watch over your life: do not let your lamps go out, and do not be unprepared, but be ready, for you do not know the hour when our Lord is coming. (2) Gather together frequently, seeking the things that benefit your souls, for all the time you have believed will be of no use to you if you are not found perfect in the last time. (3) For in the last days the false prophets and corrupters will abound, and the sheep will be turned into wolves, and love will be turned into hate. (4) For as lawlessness increases, they will hate and persecute and betray one another. And then the deceiver of the world will appear as a son of God and will perform signs and wonders, and the earth will be delivered into his hands, and he will commit abominations the likes of which have never happened before. (5) Then all humankind will come to the fiery test, and many will fall away and perish; but those who endure in their faith will be saved by the accursed one himself. (6) And then there will appear the signs of the truth: first the sign of an opening in heaven, then the sign of the sound of a trumpet, and third, the resurrection of the dead—(7) but not of all; rather, as it has been said, "The Lord will come, and all his saints with him." (8) Then the world will see the Lord coming upon the clouds of heaven. (Didache 16:1–8)[63]

The main gospel source from which Didache 16 draws is Matthew 24–25, alluding frequently to it. The first verse begins with exhortations to be ready spiritually (cf. Matt. 25:1–13, "The Ten Virgins"). In verse 2, there is a "cause and effect" warning that a lack of consistent gathering together with other believers will hinder faith-readiness. The reason for this watchfulness is given in verses 3–8, which also provide the basic chronology of the events. What follows is my summary of the content of each of the relevant sections:

> 3–4a. False prophets, corrupters, love turned into hate, law-lessness increases, persecution, and betrayal.

> 4b–5. Then the deceiver of the world (the Antichrist) will appear deceptively as a son of God, performing signs and wonders. The earth will be delivered into his hands, and he will commit unprecedented abominations (the great tribulation). Humankind will face the fiery test, and many will fall away (apostasy) and perish (martyrdom); but those who endure in their faith (true believers during the great tribulation) will be saved (delivered) by the accursed one himself (Christ).

> 6–8. And then there will appear the signs of the truth: first the sign of an opening in heaven, then the sign of the sound of a trumpet, and third, the resurrection of the dead (not the ungodly, but the righteous, cf. v. 7). Then the world will see the Lord coming upon the clouds of heaven (Shekinah-glory).

As the sequence above instructs, the Antichrist will appear first, before the coming of Christ to resurrect and deliver his faithful people. Incidentally, in two earlier chapters, the Didache interprets the elect who are gathered in Matthew 24:31 as the church: "so may your church be gathered together from the ends of the earth into your kingdom" (Didache 9:4). And, "Remember your church, Lord, to deliver it from all evil and to make it perfect in your love; and from the four winds gather the church that has been sanctified into your kingdom, which you have prepared for it" (Didache 10:5).[64] Because the Didache teaches that the church will encounter the Antichrist, it establishes the foundation of prewrath eschatology as reaching back to the apostolic period.

Our final authority is the Word of God, and that is where we must find inspired teaching for faith and practice. It is, however, wise to learn from those who have gone before us. Since church history teaches us a lot, how much more weight do writings during the apostolic age carry—such as the Didache!

Didache 16	Parallels	Matthew 24–25
1	Watchfulness	25:1–13
3a	False Prophets	24:11
3c	Diminished Love	24:12b
4a	Lawlessness Increased	24:12a
4b–d	Hate, Persecution, Betrayal	24:9–10
4e	The Antichrist	24:15a
4f	Signs and Wonders	24:24b
4g	Unequaled Tribulation	24:21
5b	Apostasy	24:10a
5c	Enduring to the End	24:13
6a–b	Sign of His Coming	24:30a
6c	Sound of the Trumpet	24:31a
6d	Resurrection-Gathering	24:31b
8a	Universal Visibility	24:30b
8b	Coming on the Clouds of Heaven	24:30c

We now turn to seven early church fathers who wrote subsequent to the Didache, all agreeing that the church will suffer the Antichrist's persecution. It will suffice to provide these seven who wrote before A.D. 250, although we could list more beyond that time period. They are given in roughly chronological order.[65]

Epistle of Barnabas (c.80–c.100)

The final stumbling-block (or source of danger) approaches. . . . We take earnest heed in these last days; for the whole [past] time of your faith will profit you nothing, unless now in this wicked time we also withstand coming sources of danger, as becometh the sons of God. That the Black One [the Antichrist] may find no means of entrance, let us flee from every vanity, let us utterly hate the works of the way of wickedness. Do not, by retiring apart, live a solitary life, as if you were already [fully] justified . . . . Take heed, lest resting at our ease, as those who are the called [of God], we should fall asleep in our sins, and the wicked prince, acquiring power over us, should thrust us away from the kingdom of the Lord. (*Epistle of Barnabas*, 4)

The Shepherd of Hermas (c.95–c.150)

[Blessed are] you who endure the great tribulation that is coming on, and [blessed are] they who shall not deny their own life. (Vision 2:2)

Those, therefore, who continue steadfast, and are put through the fire, will be purified by means of it. . . . But the white part is the age that is to come, in which the elect of God will dwell, since those elected by God to eternal life will be spotless and pure. . . . This then is the type of the great tribulation that is to come. (Vision 4:3)

Justin Martyr (c.110–c.165)

He [Jesus Christ] shall come from heaven with glory, when the man of apostasy [the Antichrist], who speaks strange things against the Most High, shall venture to do unlawful deeds on the earth against us the Christians. (*Dialogue with Trypho*, CX)

Irenaeus (c.120–c.202)

And they [the ten kings who shall arise] shall lay Babylon waste, and burn her with fire, and shall give their kingdom to the beast, and put the Church to flight. (*Against Heresies*, V, 26, 1)

And therefore, when in the end the Church shall be suddenly caught up from this, it is said, "There shall be tribulation such as has not been since the beginning, neither shall be." For this is the last contest of the righteous, in which, when they overcome they are crowned with incorruption. (*Against Heresies*, V, 29, 1)

It is therefore more certain, and less hazardous, to await the fulfillment of the prophecy [the Antichrist], than to be making surmises, and casting about for any names that may present themselves, inasmuch as many names can be found possessing the number mentioned; and the same question will, after all, remain unsolved. . . . But he indicates the number of the name now, that when this man [the Antichrist] comes we may avoid him, being aware who he is. (*Against Heresies*, V, 30, 3, 4)

For all these and other words were unquestionably spoken in reference to the resurrection of the just, which takes place after the coming of Antichrist. . . . [A]nd [with respect to] those whom the Lord shall find in the flesh, awaiting Him from heaven, and who have suffered tribulation, as well as escaped the hands of the Wicked one. (*Against Heresies*, V, 35, 1)

Tertullian (c.145–c.220)

Heresies, at the present time, will no less rend the church by their perversion of doctrine, than will Antichrist persecute her at that day by the cruelty of his attacks, except that persecution make seven martyrs, (but) heresy only apostates. (*The Prescription Against Heretics*, IV)

[A]nd that the beast Antichrist with his false prophet may wage war on the Church of God. (*On the Resurrection of the Flesh*, 25)

Now the privilege of this favour [be alive when Christ comes back] awaits those who shall at the coming of the Lord be found in the flesh, and who shall, owing to the oppressions of the time of Antichrist, deserve by an instantaneous death [i.e., raptured/translation], which is accomplished by a sudden change, to become qualified to join the rising saints; as he writes to the Thessalonians [1 Thess. 4:15–17]. (*On the Resurrection of the Flesh*, 41)

Hippolytus (c.185–c.235)

When the times are fulfilled, and the ten horns spring from the beast in the last (times), then Antichrist will appear among them. When he makes war against the saints, and persecutes them, then may we expect the manifestation of the Lord from heaven. (*On Daniel*, II, 7)

[I]n order that when those things [Antichrist's mark of the beast] come to pass, we may be prepared for them, and not deceived. For when the times advance, he too, of whom these thing are said, will be manifested. (*Treatise on Christ and Antichrist*, 50)

Now, concerning the tribulation of the persecution which is to fall upon the Church from the adversary. . . . That refers to the one thousand two hundred and threescore days (the half of the week) during which the tyrant is to reign and persecute the Church. (*Treatise on Christ and Antichrist*, 60, 61, cf. 60–67)

Cyprian (c.200–c.258)

For you ought to know and to believe, and hold it for certain, that the day of affliction has begun to hang over our heads, and the end of the world and the time of Antichrist to draw near, so that we must all stand prepared for the battle; nor consider anything but the glory of life eternal, and the crown of the confession of the Lord; and not regard those things which are coming as being such as were those which have passed away. A severer and a fiercer fight is now threatening, for which the soldiers of Christ ought to prepare themselves with uncorrupted faith and robust courage, considering that they drink the cup of Christ's blood daily, for the reason that they themselves also may be able to shed their blood for Christ. (Epistle 55, 1)

Nor let any one of you, beloved brethren, be so terrified by the fear of future persecution, or the coming of the threatening Antichrist, as not to be found armed for all things by the evangelical exhortations and precepts, and by the heavenly warnings. Antichrist is coming, but above him comes Christ also. The enemy goeth about and rageth, but immediately the Lord follows to avenge our sufferings and our wounds. The adversary is enraged and threatens, but there is One who can deliver us from his hands. (Epistle 55, 7)

These primary sources show the consistent testimony of the early church concerning the relationship between the Antichrist and the church. To be sure, not every early church father in the first two centuries wrote on this subject. However, of those who did address it, all wrote in a singular voice that the church would face the Antichrist. Prewrath agrees with the early church on this central issue, while at the same time refining related aspects on the second coming. In contrast, the pretribulational teaching had to wait more than fifteen hundred years before someone came along to introduce the concept of a so-called imminent rapture occurring before the Antichrist's arrival.

Appendix 6.
Discovery of an Ancient
Seven-Sealed Scroll

The two photographs on the following pages are of a rare fourth century B.C. Samaritan papyrus and its detached seven seals (bullae). When it was discovered in 1962 at Wadi Daliyeh, all seven seals were still fastened to the scroll. Paul Lapp describes the discovery: "This papyrus sample was part of the larger find consisting of many more fragments, some small rolls of papyrus, one still sealed with seven sealings . . ." Paul W. Lapp and Nancy L. Lapp, "An Account of the Discovery" in *Discoveries in the Wadi ed–Daliyeh*, eds., Paul W. Lapp and Nancy L. Lapp [AASOR 41] (Cambridge, MA: American Schools of Oriental Research, 1974), 5.

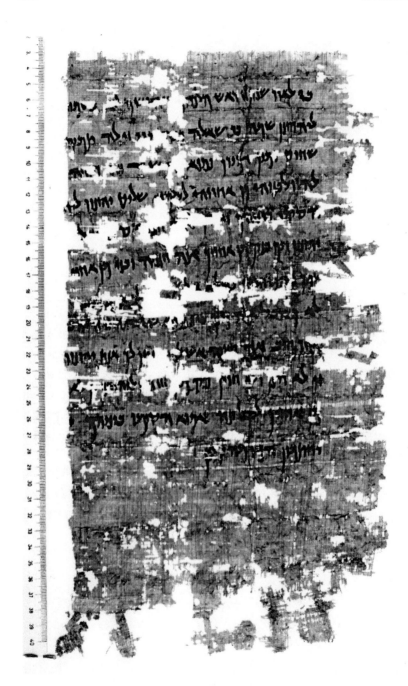

Samaritan papyrus, Wadi Daliyeh, 375-335 B.C. (Permission granted by The Israel Museum, Jerusalem and the Collection of the Israel Antiquities Authority)

Samaritan Bullae, Wadi Daliyeh, 375-335 B.C. (Permission granted by The Israel Museum, Jerusalem and the Collection of the Israel Antiquities Authority)

Notes

Part 1. The Antichrist's Great Tribulation

1. Michael W. Holmes, ed. and trans., *Apostolic Fathers: Greek Texts and English Translations*, 3rd ed., electronic ed. (Grand Rapids: Baker Books, 2007). For more early church examples, see the appendix "What Did the Early Church Believe?"

2. Nevertheless, I will mention some brief points that support why futurists such as myself understand that the last seven of the 490 years are still in the future. First, the conditions for Israel's salvation will occur when the 490 years have expired, a condition that obviously has not yet occurred: "Seventy weeks have been determined concerning your people and your holy city to put an end to rebellion, to bring sin to completion, to atone for iniquity, to bring in perpetual righteousness, to seal up the prophetic vision, and to anoint a most holy place" (Dan. 9:24). Second, Jesus cites from the 490-years passage in Daniel relating the abomination of desolation to the second coming, thereby placing it in a futurist context (Matt. 24:15; cf. Dan. 9:27; 12:11). Third, in 2 Thessalonians 2:3–4, Paul closely associates the second coming with Daniel's abomination of desolation. Fourth, the book

of Revelation relates the return of Christ to the context of the three-and-one-half years, which denotes the second half of Daniel's seven-year period (Rev. 11:2; 12:5, 6, 14; 13:5; cf. Dan. 9:27). These reasons, though not exhaustive, in my judgment provide a case that the last seven years anticipate fulfillment in the context of the Lord's coming, the time of consummation. (See Harold W. Hoehner, *Chronological Aspects of the Life of Christ* (Grand Rapids: Zondervan, 1977), 115–39.

3. The verb *gābar* is in the Hebrew hiphil stem, which expresses causative action. Ludwig Koehler and Walter Baumgartner, *The Hebrew and Aramaic Lexicon of the Old Testament*, electronic ed., trans. and ed. M. E. J. Richardson (Leiden: Brill, 2000); cf. J. G. Baldwin, *Daniel* (Downers Grove: InterVarsity, 1978), 171.

4. Pretribulationists minimize the application of the Olivet Discourse to the church. They posit a "secret rapture" occurring before the events in Matthew 24 because their theology teaches that Christ can come back at any moment to rapture the church before the Antichrist's great tribulation. Accordingly, they claim that the gathering of the elect in Matthew 24:31 does not refer to the rapture, but instead refers to the re-gathering of Israel. In addition, they interpret Jesus coming back in power and great glory in Matthew 24 as referring to the battle of Armageddon. Therefore they claim that the events described in the Olivet Discourse do not apply to the church. This theological presupposition is a forced interpretation upon the natural reading of the text. The following points support that the Olivet Discourse is, indeed, a teaching for the church.

First, in the Great Commission, Jesus taught the disciples—who are representative of the church—that he would be with them to the end of the age (Matt. 28:18–20). Jesus also taught that this end of the age extends into the events of the Olivet Discourse, since he places the end of the age inside the discourse. "And this gospel of the kingdom will be proclaimed throughout the whole world as a testimony to all nations, and then the end will come" (Matt. 24:14 ESV). Having established that the church will be present to the end of the age in verse 14, notice in verse 15

Jesus says, "Therefore when *you* see . . . ." He has the same audience in view from verses 9–14. There is no justification to claim that the "you" in verse 15 and forward is different from the "you" in verses 9–14; in other words, the church is the consistent audience of Jesus' whole discourse.

Second, it has been argued by many pretribulationists that since the gospel of Matthew is "Jewish," the Olivet Discourse cannot be for the Gentiles. This assertion is riddled with many problems: (1) The Olivet Discourse is also found in the gospels of Mark and Luke, whose audience was principally Gentile. (2) In Matthew, when Jesus was being rejected by the Jewish leadership, he taught that the gospel would expand beyond Israel to other nations: "For this reason I tell you that the kingdom of God will be taken from you and given to a people who will produce its fruit" (Matt. 21:43). Accordingly, he was *preparing* his disciples for church instruction. (3) Matthew is the only gospel that mentions the word "church," *ekklēsia* (Matt. 16:18; 18:17). This does not mean, of course, that the other gospels do not apply to the church; the point is that those who seek to disconnect church teaching from Matthew must contend with that biblical fact. (4) By their logic we should not observe the Lord's Supper since it is commanded in Matthew 26:17–30. (5) Pretribulationists agree that the Great Commission is for the church, and yet that passage is found in the book of Matthew (Matt. 28:19–20). In addition, in the Great Commission, Jesus instructs the disciples: "teaching them [new believers] to obey *everything I have commanded you.*" Why should his teaching of the Olivet Discourse and his commands therein be excluded from "everything"? Selective interpretation is a sign of a failed argument. The reasons could go on and on, but the point is that the consequences of the belief in a secret pretribulational rapture result in a tortured reading and application of Matthew 24–25. In short, it is a false dichotomy to claim that since the book of Matthew is Jewish, the Olivet Discourse does not pertain to the church. They so easily forget that the first members of the church were all Jewish, preparing to take all of Jesus' teachings and commands to the Gentiles!

Third, the early church understood that the Olivet Discourse was a teaching for the church. The Didache is arguably the earliest Christian document outside the New Testament written in the first century. The Didache stands for the longer name, "The Teaching of the Lord, by the Twelve Apostles, to Gentiles." How is this early document relevant to our subject? The Didache contains the first commentary on the Olivet Discourse, specifically on Matthew 24. In chapter 16, it explicitly teaches that the church would encounter the Antichrist; hence the reference to the "Gentiles" in the title "The Teaching of the Lord, by the Twelve Apostles, *to Gentiles.*" Further, it is noted in two earlier chapters in the Didache that the author interprets the elect who are gathered in Matthew 24:31 as the church: "so may your church be gathered together from the ends of the earth into your kingdom" (Didache 9:4); and, "Remember your church, Lord, to deliver it from all evil and to make it perfect in your love; and from the four winds gather the church that has been sanctified into your kingdom, which you have prepared for it" (Didache 10:5). Holmes, *Apostolic Fathers.* For more discussion on the relevance of the Didache, see the appendix "What Did the Early Church Believe?"

Fourth, pretribulationists claim that the rapture is not found in Matthew 24; therefore, it is argued, it cannot be a teaching for the church. Yet pretribulationists unmindfully quote the following verse to apply to the rapture: "But as for that day and hour no one knows it—not even the angels in heaven—except the Father alone." This verse is from Matthew 24:36, the Olivet Discourse! They cannot have it both ways. In addition, Matthew 24:31 contains a reference to the rapture. I will cover this latter point in Part 2.

Fifth, the description of the second coming in the Olivet Discourse is clearly parallel to Paul's teaching on the second coming in his Thessalonian epistles, which are addressed to the church; therefore, Jesus is giving church instruction. See the appendix "Parallels Between Jesus and Paul," which provides thirty parallels between Paul's teaching in the Thessalonians epistles and Jesus' Olivet Discourse, demonstrating that Paul's source for his teaching was the Olivet Discourse.

Sixth, the exhortations from Matthew 24–25 appear elsewhere in the Gospels where the disciples are representatives of the church (e.g. Luke 12:39–46; 19:11–27); and the command to the disciples from the Olivet Discourse to "watch" (*grēgoreō*) for the second coming (Matt. 24:42–43; 25:13) appears in contexts for the church to "watch" (*grēgoreō*) for the second coming (1 Thess. 5:6). Further, the thief motif that originated in Jesus' teaching (Matt. 24:42) is elsewhere applied to the church (1 Thess. 5:2, 4). Incidentally, the command to "watch" coupled with the "thief" motif is found in the same verses applied to the churches (Rev. 3:3; 16:15). *Three Views on the Rapture: Pretribulation, Prewrath, or Posttribulation*, 2nd ed., ed. Alan Hultberg (Grand Rapids: Zondervan, 2010), 220–22.

Seventh, other reasons can be given why Jesus addressed the disciples as representatives of the church. For example, the "elect" in Matthew 24 refers to Gentile and Jewish believers (i.e. the church); and a cluster of New Testament authors who wrote to local churches refer to Jesus' teaching on the second coming, applying it to their own churches. Further, the early church fathers in their writings applied Jesus' Olivet Discourse to the church. For a detailed defense of these latter three points, see Charles Cooper, *God's Elect and the Great Tribulation: An Interpretation of Matthew 24:1–31 and Daniel 9* (Bellefonte, PA: Strong Tower Publishing, 2008), 11–119.

5. Throughout this book, unless otherwise noted, Greek definitions will be from *A Greek-English Lexicon of the New Testament and Other Early Christian Literature*, rev. and ed. Fredrick W. Danker, 3rd ed. (Chicago: University of Chicago Press, 2000).

6. Daniel Wallace, *Greek Grammar Beyond the Basics: An Exegetical Syntax of the New Testament* (Grand Rapids: Zondervan, 1996), 673. However, it is possible *oun* can sometimes indicate a "transition to something new." But in our context, there is no evidence of this because the narrative clearly shows that *oun* functions to show result or inference of the spiritual action the disciples are to take from the persecution in verses 9–14; in ad-

dition, starting with verse 15, *oun* develops the agent and nature of the persecution.

7. The Greek term *thlipsis* occurs forty-five times in the New Testament: Matt. 13:21; 24:9, 21, 29; Mark 4:17; 13:19, 24; John 16:21, 33; Acts 7:10–11; 11:19; 14:22; 20:23; Rom. 2:9; 5:3(x2); 8:35; 12:12; 1 Cor. 7:28; 2 Cor. 1:4(x2), 8; 2:4; 4:17; 6:4; 7:4; 8:2, 13; Eph. 3:13; Phil. 1:17; 4:14; Col 1:24; 1 Thess. 1:6; 3:3, 7; 2 Thess. 1:4, 6; Heb. 10:33; James 1:27; Rev. 1:9; 2:9–10, 22; 7:14.

8. For further reading on the doctrine of perseverance and Scripture's warnings and exhortations and their purpose in salvation, see Thomas Schreiner, *Run to Win the Prize: Perseverance in the New Testament* (Wheaton: Crossway, 2010). For a short treatment, see his article, "Perseverance and Assurance: A Survey and a Proposal," www.sbts.edu/documents/tschreiner/2.1_article.pdf

9. In Greek grammatical terminology, the article in this context likely indicates a "well-known" sense. Daniel Wallace comments on this particular category, "The ['well-known'] article points out an object that is well known." *Greek Grammar Beyond the Basics*, 225. But this article could have an anaphoric sense, denoting a previous reference, since Paul states, "Surely you recall that I used to tell you these things while I was still with you" (2 Thess. 2:5). But the anaphoric article is broader than the well-known article and thus could include the well-known sense as well. The question Wallace says we must ask is, "*Why is it well known?*" *Greek Grammar Beyond the Basics*, 222. If the apostasy is caused by the Antichrist's great tribulation (as I will argue above), then it could be the most significant (worst) case of apostasy in Jewish or Christian history.

10. Rather than taking "God's temple" in its normal, natural, customary sense, historicist interpreters deny that Paul intends a literal, future temple in 2 Thessalonians 2:4: "He opposes and exalts himself above every so-called god or object of worship, and as a result he takes his seat in God's temple, displaying himself as God." Historicism claims that Paul's use of "temple" refers

metaphorically to the church since Paul elsewhere uses "temple" for the church. But this "church" interpretation is weak and lacks support.

Colin R. Nicholl adduces four good reasons showing that Paul has in mind a literal temple: "(1) since the author is contradicting the false eschatological claim of 2:2c, we would expect a concrete, observable and conspicuous event; (2) the use of *kathisai* ["takes his seat"] seems more naturally to suggest a literal, physical temple; (3) the definite articles clearly allude to a particular temple of the true God, which can only refer to the Jerusalem temple; (4) the immediately preceding reference to *sebasma* ["object of worship"] favours a material temple." *From Hope to Despair in Thessalonica: Situating 1 and 2 Thessalonians*, Society for New Testament Studies Monograph Series 126 (Cambridge: Cambridge University Press, 2004), 232–33, n. 34.

Daniel Wallace provides additional reasons: "It seems that by 63 CE (the date I would assign to 1 Timothy), the idiom ["God's temple"] had shifted in Christian usage sufficiently that a metaphorical nuance had become the norm. However, it is equally significant that all of the references in the Corinthian correspondence seem to require an explanation (readily supplied by Paul) in order to make the metaphorical sense clear. Thus, for Paul at least, one might chart his development as follows: 50 CE—literal notion is still in view (2 Thess 2:4). Mid-50s—metaphorical notion is developed, but the shift has to be made explicit. 60s—metaphorical notion is clearly in place, requiring no explicit referential clue for this meaning." http://bible.org/article/"temple-god"-2-thessalonians-24-literal-or-metaphorical (accessed 3/11/2012).

Finally, Gene L. Green, despite his interpretation that this is a reference to a literal temple in Thessalonica and not Jerusalem, makes an excellent point militating against a metaphorical sense of the temple being the church. He writes, "[T]he orientation of the divine claims of the "man of lawlessness" is toward the world at large and not the church." *The Letters to the Thessalonians* (Grand Rapids: Eerdmans, 2002), 312.

11. Colin R. Nicholl, "Michael, The Restrainer Removed (2 Thess. 2:6–7)," *Journal of Theological Studies* 51 (2000): 27–53. A few years later he included this article in his important work on the Thessalonian epistles, *From Hope to Despair in Thessalonica: Situating 1 and 2 Thessalonians*, Society for New Testament Studies Monograph Series 126 (Cambridge: Cambridge University Press, 2004).

12. George Eldon Ladd, *The Blessed Hope: A Biblical Study of the Second Advent and the Rapture* (Grand Rapids: Eerdmans, 1956), 6–7.

13. See the appendix, "Discovery of an Ancient Seven-Sealed Scroll," of two photographs and a brief account of the discovery of a rare fourth century B.C. seven-sealed scroll.

14. Some interpreters understand the rider on the white horse to be Christ mainly because Revelation 19:11–16 depicts the rider on a white horse, with many crowns on his head, conquering. However, the context makes this unlikely. First, it does not seem probable that the rider represents Christ since he is already active in the picture as the Lamb breaking the seal. It is incongruent to have Christ ultimately sending out himself. Second, the rider in the first seal carries a bow, while in Revelation 19, Christ is carrying a sword. Third, the rider of the first seal is wearing a wreath (*stephanos*), but in Revelation 19:12 the rider is wearing diadems (*diadēmata*). There can indeed be overlap between these two terms, but Revelation does attest to evil figures also wearing crowns, *stephanos* (Rev. 9:7). Fourth, if the first rider were Christ, there appears to be no explanation for the conspicuous lack of divine regalia compared to the plentiful regalia of Christ in Revelation 19:11–16 (although, certainly, Christ does not have to be depicted in such regalia in every instance in the book of Revelation). Fifth, it is unintelligible to have Christ allied with the other three malevolent horsemen since the seals of the four horsemen form a close literary unit. The four seals contain each of the following elements: a living creature, the command "Come!", a horse, a rider, a woe, and divine au-

thorization to carry out the woe (the third rider is the only rider lacking an authorization to carry out a woe, probably since it is a natural result of the second woe). Finally, while the first rider is carrying out conquest as humanity exalts itself, Christ will carry out vengeance at the battle of Armageddon toward the end of the bowl judgments when he alone is exalted.

It is my proposal that the conquering rider on the white horse symbolizes the Antichrist, or at least false christs of which the Antichrist would be the archetype. I also view the Antichrist not only as representing the first rider but the following three horsemen as well. In other words, the four horsemen as a whole symbolize four different malevolent *phases* of the Antichrist's campaign, the last being his supernatural revealed state starting at the midpoint. So I see them symbolizing a whole rather than disconnected entities, especially since the first four seals contain parallel elements forming a tight literary unit (Rev. 6:1–8). To be sure, the first four seals are not opened simultaneously; there is a sequential progression of the whole unfolding in phases. The following reasons are given as support for identification of the first-seal rider symbolizing the Antichrist's first phase of his malevolent campaign.

First, the book of Revelation portrays the Antichrist coming on the world scene to conquer and establish his authority: "The beast was permitted to go to war against the saints and conquer them. He was given ruling authority over every tribe, people, language, and nation" (Rev. 13:7; see also Rev. 11:7; 12:12–13:18). This will happen *before* Christ-as-conqueror comes on the scene to establish his authority with the trumpets, bowls, and Armageddon (Rev. 8–9; 15–16; 19). This point militates against seeing the first-seal rider as representing Christ, but favors it representing the Antichrist.

Second, despite my disagreement with Grant Osborne's interpretation of the rider representing human depravity, Osborne makes two important observations that better support the rider as the Antichrist. He writes, "The wording is particularly important. First, the rider is described with the unusual expression *ho kathēmenos* (the one sitting), a direct parallel to the description of God 'sitting on' the throne in 4:2, 3, 9, 10. This rider then represents humankind setting themselves up in the place of God. Next, the critical *edothē* (was given) is a divine passive pointing to God's control of the process [cf. 9:3, 5; 13:5, 7] [. . .]. It denotes the sovereign power of God over all his creation, even the forces of evil. Everything Satan and his minions do in the book occurs only by divine permission [. . .]." *Revelation* (Grand Rapids: Baker Academic, 2002), 277.

Third, the first seal likely corresponds to the first event of false christs in Jesus' Olivet Discourse because seals 2–7 correspond sequentially to events from Jesus' teaching in Matthew 24. The Antichrist's chief purpose will be to come in the name of Christ to deceive the world, so in that sense he will be the epitome of false christs. The Antichrist will be the archetypical deceiver and Christ-imitator, a theme that is developed in Revelation 12–13 and 2 Thessalonians 2:6–10. This may explain why he is coming on a white horse. White can symbolize righteousness, and since the Antichrist is coming as a counterfeit of righteousness, a white horse is fitting for his persona (cf. "And no wonder, for even Satan disguises himself as an angel of light" [2 Cor. 11:14]). However, white in combination with the horse may also symbolize strength or conquest without requiring any moral qualities, alluding to military leaders who rode white horses at times during warfare. In any event, both ideas are suitable for the Antichrist.

Fourth, in the imagery of the first seal, there are associations between Apollo and false christs/false prophecy. Apollo was a god closely associated with pagan (false) prophecy, particularly in Western Asia Minor where the book of Revelation was addressed. Allen Kerkeslager writes, "In Greco-Roman antiquity, the bow would have served as a fairly transparent symbol of Apollo, the *god who was believed to inspire prophecy*. . . . Many Jews in the Greco-Roman world were well acquainted with the imagery and motifs associated with Apollo. Philo describes how the emperor Gaius imitated Apollo by donning crowns (*stepha-*

noi) adorned with the sun's rays while carrying a bow and ar-
rows" (emphasis mine). "Apollo, Greco-Roman Prophecy, and
the Rider on the White Horse in Rev. 6:2," *Journal of Biblical Literature* 112 (1993): 118–19. Kerkeslager also explains a possible
reference to the name Apollo in Revelation 9:11: "They have as
king over them the angel of the abyss, whose name in Hebrew is
Abaddon, and in Greek, Apollyon" (119). This contextual back-
ground of allusions to Apollo adds support to the identification
of the rider as symbolizing false prophecy through false christs—
and in our Christian context, it would represent the Antichrist as
the archetype.

Given the collective reasons above, it is my preferred interpretation that the rider of the first seal symbolizes the apocalyptic antagonist to the true Christ, the Antichrist. The likely point
at which the first seal is broken will be toward the beginning of
the seven-year period. This will be the first phase of the Antichrist in his unrevealed state. He will embody deception when
he comes on the prophetic scene, making a seven-year covenant
with "the many," only to break it at the midpoint (cf. Dan. 9:27).

15. G. K. Beale, *The Book of Revelation: A Commentary on the
Greek Text* (Grand Rapids: Eerdmans, 1999), 381.

16. The Greek construction suggests that "the beasts" refers
to the Antichrist and his religious accomplice. The first three
entities, "sword, famine, and pestilence," are in the grammatical
construction called the "dative of means/instrument." The fourth
entity, "the beasts," is found in the grammatical construction
called the "ultimate agent," or, more probable in this context, the
"intermediate agent," with the ultimate agent being Death and
Hades. In other words, this indicates that the beasts are agents
themselves and may be using the sword, famine, and pestilence
as means to achieve an end. The text reads, "*apokteinai* [to kill]
en rhomphaia [with sword] *kai en limō* [and with famine] *kai en
thanatō* [and with pestilence] *kai hypo tōn thērion tēs gēs* [and
by the wild beasts of the earth]." The first three prepositional
phrases that have *en* plus the dative indicate "means/instrument."

The last prepositional phrase *hypo* plus the genitive indicates the "ultimate agent" (or possibly an intermediate agent). Wallace, *Greek Grammar Beyond the Basics*, 431–35. This is consistent with the fact that it will be Satan who will possess the Antichrist (see 2 Thess. 2:5–10; Revelation 13). We know it will be the Antichrist who will kill believers by the "sword" and prevent anyone from buying food if they do not possess his mark (Rev. 13:4–10).

17. In Greek grammatical terminology, the article in this context likely indicates a "well-known" sense. Wallace, *Greek Grammar Beyond the Basics*, 225. Another category of the article this example may fall into is the "kataphoric article." Wallace explains this second category: "The first mention, with the article, is anticipatory, followed by a phrase or statement that defines or qualifies the thing mentioned." *Greek Grammar Beyond the Basics*, 220. In this case, the beasts are qualified as those "of the earth" (cf. Rev. 13:11; Dan. 7:17).

18. See D. A. Carson, *How Long, O Lord?: Reflections on Suffering and Evil*, 2nd ed. (Grand Rapids, MI: Baker, 2006); cf. Charles Cooper, *How to Survive the Great Tribulation: Fight, Flight, or Faith* (Bellefonte, PA: Strong Tower Publishing, 2008).

Part 2. The Rapture of God's People

19. Occasionally, I hear pretribulational proponents mistakenly describe prewrath as teaching that the rapture will occur "three-quarters into the seven-year period." This is a gross misrepresentation. Prewrath teaches that the rapture will occur *sometime during the second half* of the seven-year period. It does not teach any specificity as to the timing of the rapture such as "three-quarters."

20. Johannes P. Louw and Eugene A. Nida, eds., *Greek-English Lexicon of the New Testament Based on Semantic Domains*, 2nd ed., electronic ed. (New York: United Bible Societies, 1989).

21. Ceslas Spicq, *Theological Lexicon of the New Testament*, electronic ed., trans. and ed. James D. Ernest (Peabody: Hendrickson, 1994).

22. Posttribulationism has mistakenly identified the "last trumpet" in 1 Corinthians 15:51–52 and the "trumpet of God" in 1 Thessalonians 4:16 with the seventh trumpet in Revelation 11:15. There are fundamental problems with this identification. (1) There are two unrelated purposes for Paul's parousia trumpet and the seventh trumpet. Paul's last trumpet serves the godly in *deliverance* in the resurrection and the rapture, while the seven trumpets in the book of Revelation serve the ungodly in *judgment*, with the seventh trumpet announcing the reclamation of God's kingdom. (2) The timing is different. For Paul, his last trumpet is blown immediately when Christ returns to deliver his people. In contrast, the seventh trumpet in Revelation is blown much later, after the six judgment trumpets have been blown. (3) There are two different trumpeters. It is most certain that the trumpet in 1 Corinthians 15:52 is the same "trumpet of God" in 1 Thessalonians 4:16. Accordingly, it is God who blows this special trumpet. In contrast, the seventh trumpet is blown by the seventh angel.

This brings us to the question of what Paul meant by the "*last* trumpet." The Greek term *eschatos* means "last," which can carry a few applications. It is often assumed that the term in the expression "the last trumpet" denotes a final item in a series of trumpets. But the context in 1 Corinthians 15 shows no hint of a series of trumpets. Only one trumpet is in view. Further, in this same chapter on the resurrection, Paul uses *eschatos* to refer to *the final item* in three series of categories: the resurrected Jesus appearing last to Paul (1 Cor. 15:6–8), abolishing the last enemy (1 Cor. 15:24–26), and the last Adam (1 Cor. 15:45). In those three events, Paul does not just list the last item but mentions other items within its series. However, when he mentions the last trumpet, he does not make any reference to previous trumpets. This suggests that Paul intends another sense of *eschatos* for the "last trumpet." Since the resurrection represents the climactic redemptive event when Christ comes back, Paul likely has in mind "last" in the sense of signifying that the present order is no more, implying that a new era has dawned in God's redemptive work. Paul may also be alluding to the common purpose of the blowing of a trumpet in the Old Testament to gather or assemble God's people. Thus, Paul sees the resurrection of God's people as the eschatological gathering. Incidentally, *eschatos* can also carry the meaning of utmost or finest, which carries the connotation of culmination. Either of these latter senses is much more plausible than the posttribulational interpretation, which sees it as referring to the seventh trumpet in the book of Revelation. Incidentally, the term for "trumpet" is *salpigx*, which can denote simply the sound of the trumpet blast or the instrument itself. This will not be the only eschatological trumpet associated with the Lord's coming. For example, a trumpet blast announces the day of the Lord's wrath (Joel 2:1); trumpet blasts sound during the day of the Lord's wrath (Zeph. 1:15–16; cf. Rev. 8:2); and a trumpet blast calls refugees from Assyria and Egypt back home to Israel (Isa. 27:12–13; Zech. 9:14–16).

23. *Paul and the Parousia: An Exegetical and Theological Investigation* (Peabody: Hendrickson, 1997), 82.

24. Matt. 11:12; 12:29; 13:19; John 6:15; 10:12, 28–29; Acts 8:39; 23:10; 2 Cor. 12:2, 4; 1 Thess. 4:17; Jude 1:23; Rev. 12:5.

25. The Septuagint (abbreviated LXX) is an ancient Greek translation of the Old Testament made for Greek-speaking Jews. The LXX does not use *harpazō* to translate the Hebrew *lāqah*. It uses the term *metatithēmi*, which means in this context "to convey from one place to another, put in another place, transfer." The author of Hebrews consistently uses *metatithēmi* twice of the Enoch event. "By faith Enoch was taken up [*metatithēmi*] so that he did not see death, and he was not to be found because God took him up [*metatithēmi*]. For before his removal [*metathesis*] he had been commended as having pleased God" (Heb. 11:5). In addition, the term for "removal" in this verse is the noun form of the previous verb *metathesis*, which means in this instance "re-

moval to another place." So these terms in this particular context are used to indicate a rapture. Moreover, in describing Enoch's rapture, extra-biblical literature uses *harpazō* (Wis. 4.10–11; 2 *Enoch* 3.1). Incidentally, some have claimed that Enoch actually did die, citing Hebrews 11:13: "These all died in faith...." But the "all" must be interpreted in its context. The author of Hebrews explicitly qualifies an exception to the faithful heroes who died: "By faith Enoch was taken up *so that he did not see death,* and he was not to be found because God took him up. For before his removal he had been commended as having pleased God" (Heb. 11:5, emphasis mine).

26. There is a theological question about the abode of Old Testament saints (those who had died) before Christ's resurrection; hence there is a question about whether Enoch and Elijah went directly to heaven in the Father's presence or whether they dwelled in another place. That is beyond the scope of this discussion, but we can be most certain that Old Testament saints did enjoy a state of fellowship, joy, and comfort, which is inferred from the biblical examples of Moses and Elijah (Matt. 17:3) and Abraham and Lazarus (Luke 16:25).

27. Many pretribulationists argue that those who are taken are taken to judgment, and those who are left are left for deliverance. Specifically, this pretribulational interpretation views those who are taken as being the ones taken for judgment after the battle of Armageddon and those who are left as being the ones who survive the day of the Lord and enter the millennial kingdom. This interpretation, however, violates the natural reading of the passage. Their argument is based mainly on the Noahic illustration in verses 37–39. They contend that the judgment "the flood came and took them [the wicked] all away" parallels the event of "one will be taken." However, identifying "the wicked" with "those who will be taken" is mistaken for the following reasons:

First, the domestic and agricultural illustrations in verses 40–41 (men in the field and women grinding grain) parallel the Noahic illustration, so they are not intended to *illustrate the illus-*

tration of the Noah illustration in verses 37–39. Instead, verses 40–41 intend to illustrate the gathering of God's people at the parousia (Matt. 24:30–31). At the separation when the parousia begins in verse 31, who is being taken? It is God's elect, not the wicked—the whole point of invoking the illustration.

Second, the pretribulational schema breaks the parallelism of the illustrations. When the text is examined, however, we see that the delivery of Noah's family is described first ("the day when Noah entered the ark" v. 38), and the judgment upon the ungodly is described second ("the flood came and swept them all away" v. 39). To preserve the parallel, a man in the field and a woman grinding at the mill are taken (delivered), then the other man in the field and other woman grinding at the mill are left (judgment).

Third, some translations render the action of the flood illustration in verse 39 as "the flood came and took them [the wicked] all away." The rendering "took" is unfortunate because unsuspecting readers may assume it is the same "taken" used in verses 40–41. There are two different Greek terms behind the English that contain nearly opposite meanings. The English Standard Version recognizes this and accordingly replaces "took" with "swept away" ("and they were unaware until the flood came and swept them all away, so will be the coming of the Son of Man," Matt. 24:39 ESV). The Greek term in verse 39 is *airō*, which in this particular context of the judgment-flood illustration means to "take away, remove." In contrast, the Greek term in verses 40–41 is *paralambanō*, carrying the sense of intimate receiving. Some claim that *paralambanō* does not always carry the sense of receiving in a positive sense. This is true, but misleading. Of the forty-nine times this term is used in the New Testament, it is used only three times negatively (Matt. 27:27, John 19:16, Acts 23:18). This rare negative sense is found in a specific narrow context of a prisoner being handed over to the jurisdiction of soldiers, a context not relevant to the parousia. It is a strained lexical argument to apply this unlikely meaning to our target passage. On this fallacy, see D. A. Carson, *Exegetical Fallacies*, 2nd ed. (Grand Rapids: Baker, 1996), 37–41.

Fourth, in verses 40–41, the term for "taken" is *paralambanō,* which conveys a positive receiving. This receiving is contrasted with the one who is "left." The Greek term behind "left" is *aphiēmi,* which in this context means "to move away, with the implication of causing a separation, leave, depart from." So we have a Greek positive term for "taken" contrasted with a Greek negative term for "left"; therefore, the one who is "left" is more in keeping with the idea of separation and judgment than deliverance. Not surprisingly, *just a few days later,* Jesus used *paralambanō* when he reassured his disciples that at his return, he would take them to be with him: "And if I go and make ready a place for you, I will come again and take [*paralambanō*] you to be with me, so that where I am you may be too" (John 14:3). It is the same context (Christ's return), the same audience (his disciples), and the same terminology (*paralambanō*).

Finally, in the same parousia context, Jesus provides another illustration for being prepared for his coming (Matt. 25:1–13). The five wise virgins who were prepared are taken to be with the bridegroom; the five foolish ones who were not prepared are left. Accordingly, the parable of the ten virgins is consistent with verses 37–41, supporting our interpretation that those who are taken are taken for deliverance and those who are left are left for judgment.

These five reasons demonstrate that the ones who are taken are the righteous for deliverance and the ones who are left are the wicked for judgment.

28. I want to clear up a common assumption. It has erroneously been assumed by many that the second coming begins with the battle of Armageddon. Instead, the parousia begins with Christ's appearance in the clouds to deliver his people, followed by the day of the Lord's wrath executed through the trumpet judgments, followed by the bowl judgments and Armageddon. At the rapture, the souls of believers who have died come with Christ to *receive* their new bodies. It is a deliverance event (1 Thess. 4:14). In contrast, at Armageddon, the resurrected believers come with Christ *already in* their new

bodies. It is a judgment event. "The armies that are in heaven, *dressed in white, clean, fine linen,* were following him on white horses" (Rev. 19:14, emphasis mine). We know that these armies are believers because we are told a few verses earlier that it is the bride (i.e. believers): "Let us rejoice and exult and give him glory, because the wedding celebration of the Lamb has come, and his bride has made herself ready. She was permitted to be dressed in *bright, clean, fine linen*" (*for the fine linen is the righteous deeds of the saints*)" (Rev. 19:7–8, emphasis mine). In one instance in Revelation, angels are depicted wearing similar attire (Rev. 15:6) and the saints are seen wearing white (Rev. 3:4–5, 18; 6:11; 7:9, 13–14; 19:7–8). The context of the redemptive marriage supper joins the bride with the Lamb; and we see the bride and the Lamb going to battle against their enemies, resulting in a judgment supper: "Then I saw an angel standing in the sun, and with a loud voice he called to all the birds that fly directly overhead, 'Come, gather for the great supper of God, to eat the flesh of kings, the flesh of captains, the flesh of mighty men, the flesh of horses and their riders, and the flesh of all men, both free and slave, both small and great'" (Rev. 19:17–18 ESV). Moreover, we are told elsewhere that accompanying the Lamb to battle are the saints: "They will make war with the Lamb, but the Lamb will conquer them, because he is Lord of lords and King of kings, and those accompanying the Lamb are the called, chosen, and faithful" (Rev. 17:14). Therefore, these reasons show that the armies that follow Jesus into battle in Revelation 19:14 are most certainly saints, not angels. To be sure, this is not to say that angels will not also accompany Jesus into battle. They likely will, since executing his judgments is a role for angels. But in this particular verse, the armies refer to the redeemed saints.

29. For further argumentation that shows the 144,000 is not the church, see *Three Views on the Rapture*, 144–46.

30. For further argumentation that shows this group is the church and/or including all of God's people, see *Three Views on the Rapture*, 129–37.

31. In addition, the early church, according to the Didache, interpreted the elect who are gathered in Matthew 24:31 as the church: "so may your church be gathered together from the ends of the earth into your kingdom" (Didache 9:4); and, "Remember your church, Lord, to deliver it from all evil and to make it perfect in your love; and from the four winds gather the church that has been sanctified into your kingdom, which you have prepared for it" (Didache 10:5). Holmes, *Apostolic Fathers.*

Part 3. The Day of the Lord's Wrath

32. Jeffrey J. Niehaus, *God at Sinai: Covenant & Theophany in the Bible and Ancient Near East* (Grand Rapids: Zondervan, 1995), 157; Meredith G. Kline, "Primal Parousia," *Westminster Theological Journal* 40 (1978): 245–80.

33. Niehaus, *God at Sinai*, 18.

34. Kline, "Primal Parousia," 245–70.

35. Cf. Asher Intrater, *Who Ate Lunch With Abraham* (Peoria: Intermedia, 2011).

36. The expression "day of the Lord" (*yôm yhwh*) is found in the Old Testament sixteen times: Joel 1:15; 2:1, 11; 2:31; 3:14; Obad. 1:15; Isa. 13:6, 9; Ezek. 13:5; Amos 5:18(x2), 20; Zeph. 1:7, 14(x2); Mal. 4:5. Half of these instances refer to a historically fulfilled day-of-the-Lord judgment against Judah or Israel: Isa. 13:6; Ezek. 13:5; Joel 1:15; 2:1, 11; Amos 5:18(x2), 20. The other half refer to the eschatological day of the Lord upon all the nations: Isa. 13:9; Joel 2:31; 3:14; Obad. 1:15; Zeph. 1:7, 14(x2); Mal. 4:5. See also Isa. 2:12; 13:13; 34:8; Ezek. 7:19; 30:3; Zeph. 1:8, 18; 2:2–3; Zech. 14:7; Lam. 1:12; 2:1.

37. This is called the "word-concept" fallacy, an assumption that studying a single word or phrase corresponds to having studied the entire biblical concept. The fallacy is also called the "concordance" method of interpretation. One should not simply open up a concordance and finger down the page looking for us-

ages of a single word and stop there. It can be a beginning point for study, but there is an important difference between studying a biblical concept and studying the range of meanings of a single word. For example, if we want to learn what the Bible teaches about love, it would be a mistake to restrict our study only to the word *agapē* because there are many terms describing different aspects of love. We need to take Scripture in a normal, natural, contextual sense and recognize synonyms and other similar phrases that describe a concept rather than collapsing an entire concept into a single term. Moisés Silva gives this additional example: "A very important passage on the subject of hypocrisy is Isaiah 1:10–15, but the student suckled at the concordance would never find [the word "hypocrisy"]; instead, he would come to an unrefined understanding of the topic." *Biblical Words and Their Meaning: An Introduction to Lexical Semantics*, rev. ed. (Grand Rapids: Zondervan, 1994), 27. See also D. A. Carson, "Word-Study Fallacies," in *Exegetical Fallacies*, 2nd ed. (Grand Rapids: Baker Books, 1996), 27–64. Therefore, we must be careful not to assume if a passage lacks the exact expression "day of the Lord," it must not be referring to God's eschatological judgment.

38. Donald K. Campbell and Jeffrey L. Townsend, eds., *The Coming Millennial Kingdom: A Case for Premillennial Interpretation* (Grand Rapids: Kregel, 1997); Robert L. Saucy, "Part Four: The Place of Israel," in *The Case for Progressive Dispensationalism: The Interface Between Dispensational & Non-Dispensational Theology* (Grand Rapids: Zondervan, 1993); Barry E. Horner, *Future Israel: Why Christian Anti-Judaism Must Be Challenged* (Nashville: B&H Academic, 2007); Walter C. Kaiser Jr., *The Promise-Plan of God: A Biblical Theology of the Old and New Testament* (Grand Rapids: Zondervan, 2008).

39. For more on Jesus' Jewish context, see Michael L. Brown, *The Real Kosher Jesus* (Lake Mary, FL: Frontline, 2012).

40. Greg A. King, "The Day of the Lord in Zephaniah," *Bibliotheca Sacra* 152 (January–March 1995): 18.

41. *Three Views on the Rapture*, 202.

42. In addition, Colin R. Nicholl provides six reasons 1 Thessalonians 5:1–11 is closely linked to 4:13–18: "(1) Both relate to the fate of believers at the eschaton and both reflect an 'apocalyptic' conceptual framework; (2) they have a similar structure: the topic statement with *adelphoi* (4:13; 5:1), the essential reply (4:14; 5:2) and the paraenetic conclusion (4:18; 5:11); (3) 5:10's *eite katheudōmen* recalls 4:13–18, while *eite grēgorōmen* seems to allude to the problem underlying 5:11ff.; (4) Jesus' death and resurrection are the basis for confidence regarding eschatological destiny in both (4:14a; 5:9–10); (5) 'being with Christ' is the eschatological goal in both (4:17b; 5:10); (6) both have the same function of reassuring/encouraging the community members (4:18; 5:11), and indeed 5:11 may well function to conclude 4:13ff." *From Hope to Despair in Thessalonica*, 73.

43. This is an important distinction because pretribulationism identifies Jesus' and Paul's use of birth pangs with the same event, thereby making the day of the Lord's wrath the great tribulation. But this is flawed for six reasons:

1. Paul's usage is found at the inception of the day of the Lord; Jesus' usage in Matthew 24 occurs before the great tribulation. In other words, Jesus uses the birthing metaphor to warn that the end has *not arrived* ("Make sure that you are not alarmed, for this must happen, but the end is still to come. . . . All these things are the beginning of birth pains"). Paul uses it to announce that the end *has arrived* ("then sudden destruction comes on them, like labor pains," 1 Thess. 5:3; cf. Isa. 13:7–8).

2. Jesus emphasizes that while the beginning of birth pains is extremely difficult (Matt. 24:8), it is *tolerable*; hence the reason he can reassure his disciples: "Make sure that you are not alarmed, for this must happen, but the end is still to come" (Matt. 24:6). In contrast, Paul is drawing from Isaiah's labor imagery focused on the *intolerable* stage

of actual giving birth: "[C]ramps and pain seize hold of them like those of a woman who is straining to give birth" (Isa. 13:8).

3. Jesus teaches that the "beginning of birth pangs" is what the last generation of believers are *destined* to experience (Matt. 24:4–8); Paul teaches the opposite, that the last generation of believers is promised *exemption* from the hard labor pains, the time of God's wrath (1 Thess. 5:9).

4. The labor pains in Matthew 24 refer to *natural* events, such as false christs, wars, famines, and earthquakes (Matt. 24:5–8). Paul's reference is to the *supernatural* event of the day of the Lord (citing Isaiah 13:6–10; cf. 2 Thess. 1:5–8).

5. Jesus' beginning of birth pangs occurs *before* the celestial disturbances (Matt. 24:8–29). In the passage Paul is drawing from, Isaiah associates the birth pangs with the celestial disturbance of the *onset* of the day of the Lord (Isa. 13:8–10).

6. Jesus uses the birthing metaphor to apply to both unbelievers and believers (Matt. 24:5–8). Paul applies it exclusively to unbelievers (1 Thess. 5:3–4).

44. For more on Paul's main purpose in 1 Thessalonians 5:1–11, see Nicholl, *From Hope to Despair*, 67–79.

45. One of the most debated verses in the book is Revelation 3:10: "Because you have kept my admonition to endure steadfastly, I will also keep you from the hour of testing that is about to come on the whole world to test those who live on the earth." Without minimizing the importance of the exegesis, I would like to step back and give a simple response, especially to the way pretribulationism interprets this verse. Pretribulationism reads this as a promise to the church being raptured ("keep you from") before the day of the Lord's wrath ("the hour of testing"). This is supposed to prove a pretribulational rapture. However, there is a flaw if they think they "own" this conclusion: Prewrath also

affirms that the rapture will happen before the day of the Lord. The hour of testing as the day of the Lord's wrath only proves that the church will not experience this wrath (cf. 1 Thess. 5:9). Revelation 3:10 does not address the fundamental question of *when* the day of the Lord begins. The verse only gives a promise of a particular protection. As for when God's wrath begins, we must look elsewhere in Scripture. Therefore, this verse is moot on the rapture question.

46. G. K. Beale, who, despite interpreting the book of Revelation from a historicist framework, cites helpful extra-biblical Jewish literature that suggests that the silence serves as a revelatory announcement of judgment by God. For example, one particular text he cites showing the connection between silence and the verdict and execution of judgment is *Zohar* 3, Shemoth 4a–4b: "And the books are open. At this hour and moment [when] the Lord ascends to his throne . . . the singing ceases and silence falls. Judgment begins. . . . Angelic companions [again] fearlessly sing . . . [and again] the voices are silent. Then rises the Lord from the judgment throne." *The Book of Revelation: A Commentary on the Greek Text,* The New International Greek Testament Commentary (Grand Rapids: Eerdmans, 1999), 452.

47. Louw and Nida, *Greek-English Lexicon of the New Testament.*

48. Beale, *The Book of Revelation,* 491–93.

49. Louw and Nida, *Greek-English Lexicon of the New Testament.*

50. On this issue, I am indebted to Steven Lancaster and his personal correspondence, as well as his permission to use his comments here on the meaning and location of Armageddon. Lancaster is director of Biblical Backgrounds (http://www.bibback.com/).

51. *Contra* Charles C. Torrey who has argued that *Harmagedōn* is the transliteration of the Hebrew *har mô 'ēd* ("mountain of assembly"), referring to Mount Zion/Jerusalem (cf. Isa. 14:12–14). "Armageddon," *Harvard Theological Review* 31 (1938): 237–48.

This is unlikely because it is a conjectural emendation, i.e., lacks textual manuscript evidence.

52. This parenthetical exhortation in Revelation 16:15 is not intended to give a temporal indicator as to when the Lord will return. It does not mean his parousia has not occurred up to this point with the church still on earth (*contra* posttribulationism). Nor does it mean that his parousia will begin at Armageddon. It is a mistake to read into the expression "I come like a thief" as meaning he has not yet returned. It is simply a reminder for the reader (or hearer) not to lose spiritual vigilance. This parenthetical warning within the apocalyptic narrative instructs us that those who are not spiritually watchful when the Lord returns will find themselves shamefully on the wrong side, lest they experience the day of the Lord's wrath. The spiritually watchful, however, will find themselves fighting alongside the divine alliance. "[The kings of the world] will make war with the Lamb, but the Lamb will conquer them, because he is Lord of lords and King of kings, and those accompanying the Lamb are the called, chosen, and faithful" (Rev. 17:14).

53. See Cooper, *God's Elect and the Great Tribulation*, 33–51. See also Mike Coldagelli, http://www.signetringministries.org/2013/04/28/1186/ (accessed 6/5/13), and D. Ragan Ewing, http://bible.org/seriespage/chapter-4-evidence-jerusalem-harlot (accessed 6/12/13).

Appendixes

54. Matt. 24:3, 27, 37, 39; 1 Cor. 15:23; 16:17; 2 Cor. 7:6–7; 10:10; Phil 1:26; 2:12; 1 Thess. 2:19; 3:13; 4:15; 5:23; 2 Thess. 2:1, 8–9; James 5:7–8; 2 Pet. 1:16; 3:4, 12; 1 John 2:28.

55. There are more co-referential instances for Paul: Salvation will occur at the day of the Lord/parousia (1 Cor. 5:5; 15:23); boasting in labor will occur at the day of the Lord/parousia (Phil. 2:16; 1 Thess. 2:19); and events will transpire before the day of the Lord/parousia (2 Thess. 2:1–3). *From Hope to Despair in*

Thessalonica, 51, n. 13; and L. J. Kreitzer, *Jesus and God in Paul's Eschatology* (Sheffield: JSOT, 1987), 112–29.

56. *Four Views on the Book of Revelation*, ed. C. Marvin Pate (Grand Rapids: Zondervan, 1998).

57. The Greek construction in this verse is ambiguous. It could be translated, "Therefore write what you have seen, *that is,* what is, and what will happen after these things." This may be what is intended since the last two clauses seem to function as explanatory to the first clause.

58. For debate on whether the particular harvest mentioned in Revelation 14:14–16 depicts the rapture or a judgment harvest, see *Three Views on the Rapture,* 134–35.

59. Malachi 4:5 relates to the eschatological day of the Lord. Yet does not Jesus identify this prophecy as already being fulfilled in the coming of John the Baptist, thereby rendering any expectation of a future literal coming of Elijah unnecessary? "For all the prophets and the law prophesied until John appeared. And if you are willing to accept it, he is Elijah, who is to come" (Matt. 11:13–14; cf. 17:10–13). There are some things to consider.

First, since Jesus envisioned his ministry in two phases— redemption and reigning—it makes sense when he says that while Elijah has already come (John the Baptist the precursor), Elijah will also come in the future. "He answered, 'Elijah does indeed come first and will restore all things. And I tell you that Elijah has already come'" (Matt. 17:11–12). It is noteworthy that Jesus said this after John the Baptist had died, indicating a future aspect of the coming of Elijah.

Second, it is confirmed by Gabriel that John the Baptist does not fulfill the coming of Elijah in a literal sense but in a typological sense: "And he will go as forerunner before the Lord *in the spirit and power of Elijah*, to turn the hearts of the fathers back to their children and the disobedient to the wisdom of the just, to make ready for the Lord a people prepared for him" (Luke 1:17, emphasis mine). Darrell L. Bock observes, "Luke's 'like Elijah' position may serve to clarify Matthew and Mark in that there also continued to exist in Christian circles the hope of Elijah's return at the end, when God will do his final eschatological work. . . . Luke may have feared a misunderstanding that an Elijah identification for John the Baptist would represent a denial of this future Elijah, who is associated in Malachi with the decisive day of the Lord. . . . What Jesus says in Matt 17 and what Luke says here is there is a pattern of ministry like that of Elijah into which John the Baptist fits, without denying that in the end Elijah will return. This dual use of the Elijah motif fits the 'already-not yet' tension present in so much of NT eschatology." *Luke: 1:1–9:50*, Baker Exegetical Commentary on the New Testament (Grand Rapids: Baker Academic, 1994), 902.

Third, in John's Gospel, we are told that when the Jewish leaders asked John the Baptist if he were the Elijah to come, John answered in the exclamatory negative, "So they asked him, 'Then who are you? Are you Elijah?' He said, 'I am not!' 'Are you the Prophet?' He answered, 'No!'" (John 1:21). The only natural way to understand that Elijah has already come but has not already come is to view it with Jesus' two-phase coming: John the Baptist came in the "spirit and power" of Elijah at Christ's first coming, with a literal fulfillment of Elijah unfolding in proximity to Christ's second coming as a sign preceding the day of the Lord (Mal. 4:5).

Fourth, a case could be made that one of the two witnesses in Revelation will be Elijah. The powers granted to these witnesses are described as follows: "These two have the power to close up the sky so that it does not rain during the time they are prophesying" (Rev. 11:6). This is the pattern of power Elijah possessed (1 Kings 17:1; James 5:17).

Fifth, Elijah is one of the few Old Testament figures who did not experience death: "As they were walking along and talking, suddenly a fiery chariot pulled by fiery horses appeared. They went between Elijah and Elisha, and Elijah went up to heaven in a windstorm" (2 Kings 2:11). This could suggest an aspect of his purpose for coming again.

Sixth, in the Transfiguration, a few of Jesus' disciples witnessed a preview of Elijah being associated with Christ's coming in future glory. This is the same context in which Jesus tells his disciples that Elijah is coming (Matt. 16:27–17:13). Therefore, it is maintained that John the Baptist functioned in the pattern of ministry like Elijah, yet there is a real, future expectation of Elijah before the day of the Lord. This point is important because on the very same day the rapture takes place, the day of the Lord's wrath begins to unfold. Since Elijah is a precursor to the day of the Lord, the logical inference is that he will appear sometime before the rapture. Accordingly, the prophecy of Elijah establishes Christ's coming as expectant, not imminent. This point is often missed in pretribulational literature. Incidentally, there is nothing that requires Elijah's entire ministry to be completed before the day of the Lord begins—only that it must commence beforehand (*Contra* Robert H. Gundry, *The Church and the Tribulation* [Grand Rapids: Zondervan, 1973], 94).

60. We could add a fifth prophetic event that must occur before the day of the Lord: the unbelieving world saying, "Peace and security!" In his first epistle to the Thessalonians, Paul taught that the world, oblivious to the impending wrath, will be uttering this slogan before the day of the Lord. "Now when they are saying, 'There is peace and security,' then sudden destruction comes on them, like labor pains on a pregnant woman, and they will surely not escape" (1 Thess. 5:3).

61. *Prosdechomai* is found fourteen times in the New Testament: Mark 15:43; Luke 2:25, 38; 12:36; 15:2; 23:51; Acts 23:21; 24:15; Rom. 16:2; Phil. 2:29; Titus 2:13; Heb. 10:34; 11:35; Jude 1:21.

62. The two works that pioneered the prewrath position were Marvin Rosenthal, *The Pre-Wrath Rapture of the Church* (Nashville: Thomas Nelson, 1990), and Robert Van Kampen, *The Sign* (Wheaton: Crossway Books, 1992).

63. Holmes, *Apostolic Fathers.*

64. Holmes, *Apostolic Fathers.*

65. *The Ante-Nicene Fathers, Translations of the Writings of the Fathers down to A.D. 325,* Vol. 1, eds. Alexander Roberts and James Donaldson (Grand Rapids: Eerdmans, 1979).

Scripture Index

About the Author

Alan Kurschner is director of Eschatos Ministries, dedicated to teaching biblical eschatology from a futurist, premillennial, prewrath perspective. Kurschner holds an M.A. in biblical languages from Gordon-Conwell Theological Seminary.

For more resources, visit Eschatos Ministries:
www.AlanKurschner.com

CPSIA information can be obtained at www.ICGtesting.com
Printed in the USA
LVOW08*1648041213

363494LV00001BA/5/P

9 780985 363307